W9-CAJ-396

MILESTONES

IN MODERN
WORLD HISTORY

The Mexican
Revolution

MILESTONES
IN MODERN
WORLD HISTORY

MILESTONES
IN MODERN
WORLD HISTORY

1600 · · · 1750 · ·   · · · · 1940 · · · 2000

The
Mexican
Revolution

LOUISE CHIPLEY SLAVICEK

CHELSEA HOUSE
An Infobase Learning Company

The Mexican Revolution

Chelsea House
An imprint of Infobase Learning
132 West 31st Street
New York, NY 10001

Library of Congress Cataloging-in-Publication Data

Slavicek, Louise Chipley, 1956–
The Mexican Revolution / by Louise Chipley Slavicek.
 p. cm. — (Milestones in modern world history)
Includes bibliographical references and index.
ISBN 978-1-60413-459-9 (hardcover)
1. Mexico—History—Revolution, 1910-1920—Juvenile literature. 2. Mexico—History—20th century—Juvenile literature. I. Title. II. Series.

F1234.S628 2011
972.08'1—dc22   2010026902

Chelsea House books are available at special discounts when purchased in bulk quantities for businesses, associations, institutions, or sales promotions. Please call our Special Sales Department in New York at (212) 967-8800 or (800) 322-8755.

You can find Chelsea House on the World Wide Web at http://www.chelseahouse.com.

Text design by Erik Lindstrom
Cover design by Alicia Post
Composition by Keith Trego
Cover printed by Bang Printing, Brainerd, MN
Book printed and bound by Bang Printing, Brainerd, MN
Date printed: March 2011
Printed in the United States of America

Printed in the United States of America
10 9 8 7 6 5 4 3 2 1

This book is printed on acid-free paper.

All links and Web addresses were checked and verified to be correct at the time of publication. Because of the dynamic nature of the Web, some addresses and links may have changed since publication and may no longer be valid.

CONTENTS

1

The First Great Social Revolution

The Mexican Revolution is neither the most famous nor the most radical of the great social revolutions of the twentieth century, but it does have the distinction of being the first. Seven years before the Bolshevik Revolution shook Russia in 1917, nearly four decades before the success of the Communist Chinese Revolution in 1949, and nearly a half-century before the Cuban Revolution of 1959, what was destined to be the largest and deadliest social upheaval in Latin American history erupted in Mexico.

When the Mexican Revolution began in November 1910, the goals of its top leadership were strictly political. Francisco Madero, the wealthy landowner and political reformer who launched the revolution, was uninterested in changing Mexico's social and economic fabric. Rather, it was his deep faith in democratic principles and the rule of law that drove Madero to rebel. For nearly 35 years, Mexico's autocratic leader, President Porfirio Díaz, had relied on election fraud, bribery, and intimidation to subvert Mexico's democratic constitution and remain in power. In 1910, despite an earlier pledge to retire from politics, the 80-year-old president brazenly rigged yet another national election to secure his eighth term in office. To ensure victory, Díaz even had Madero, his main opponent in the race, thrown into prison during the campaign's final weeks. Madero finally decided that he—and Mexico—had had enough of Díaz's despotic ways. Fleeing across the border into Texas, he called on the Mexican people to rise up against their president on November 20, 1910.

By early 1911, tens of thousands of Mexicans had answered Madero's call to arms. Among them were upper- and middle-class landowners and businessmen like Madero, who sought to change Mexico's corrupt and undemocratic political leadership—but not its basic social or economic structures. The backbone of Madero's revolutionary army, however, was made up of the poor peasants and workers who constituted the vast majority of Mexico's population, and they viewed the rebellion's chief aims very differently.

Madero's impoverished foot soldiers saw in the revolution a chance to finally reverse the policies of Díaz's strongly pro-business and pro-hacendado (large landowner) regime and create a more equitable society. Determined to turn Mexico into a world power, Díaz made the rapid modernization and expansion of the nation's economy his top priority. Unfortunately, the break-neck pace of Mexico's industrial and agricultural development under Díaz had come at an enormous cost to the country's vast lower class. During his long tenure, the gap between Mexico's haves and have-nots widened to a record chasm. Big commercial planters were given virtually free rein to seize peasant lands, and government troops crushed strikes initiated by underpaid factory and mine workers. Consequently, what drove the rank

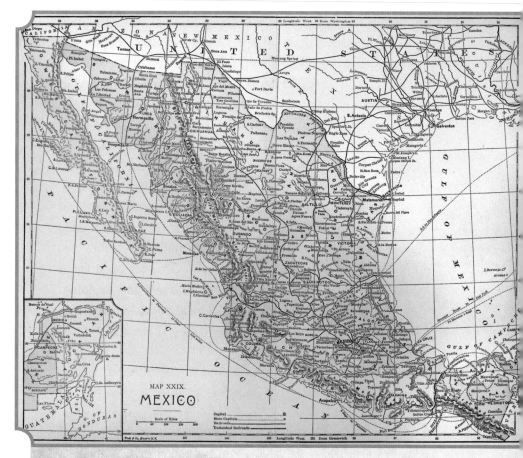

A period map of Mexico in the early 1900s, showing the nation's individual states. The Mexican Revolution, which lasted from 1910 to 1920, was characterized by several movements and changed from a revolt against the established order to a multisided civil war.

and file of Madero's army to risk their lives on the battlefield was much more than just a desire for political "freedom," as the socially conservative Madero wanted to believe.[1] Rather it was the hope that a victorious Madero would reward their battlefield sacrifices by restoring lost peasant lands, guaranteeing workers a living wage, and enacting other sweeping social reforms.

By June 1911, under the skillful direction of such men as the zealous land reformer Emiliano Zapata and the colorful bandit-turned-warrior Pancho Villa, Madero's rebel army had routed Díaz's forces, and the deposed president was on his way to exile in Europe. A few months later, Madero won the presidency by a landslide in the first truly free elections held in Mexico in more than a third of a century. As far as Madero was concerned, the revolution was over; now it was time to focus on building a stronger Mexican nation by resuming the rapid industrial and agricultural development of the Díaz years. With that goal in mind, Madero insisted that any land redistribution, labor, or other social reforms be limited and gradual, at least for the foreseeable future. Unsurprisingly, this did not play well with the downtrodden masses that had helped put him in power in the first place. By 1912, Mexico was once again plunged into violence, as land-hungry peasants and exploited workers joined forces with ambitious local politicians to overthrow Madero.

A LONG, CHAOTIC, AND BLOODY UPHEAVAL

For the next eight years, Mexico was plagued by nearly constant warfare as a series of revolutionary and counter revolutionary leaders—many more interested in securing power for themselves than in solving the problems of the Mexican people—vied for control of the nation. In 1920, a full decade after Madero had called on Mexicans to rise up against the tyrannical Díaz, the inauguration of the popular revolutionary general Álvaro Obregón as Mexico's president finally brought a halt to the unrelenting violence and political turmoil.

Between 1 million and 1.5 million Mexicans are thought to have died as a result of the Mexican Revolution of 1910–1920. Perhaps a third of the revolution's victims perished in battle or were executed. Most of the rest succumbed to influenza, typhus, and other infectious diseases, which rapidly spread through a population weakened by war-related food shortages and incessant violence. Despite the terrible toll it exacted on the Mexican people, the revolution failed to eliminate the country's grinding poverty or create a genuinely egalitarian social order. Nonetheless, it did inspire the creation of one of the most socially progressive political documents of all time, the Constitution of 1917, which governs Mexico even today. Some of the constitution's most revolutionary guarantees are still a long way from being realized, such as the right of all Mexicans to enjoy a basic minimum standard of living. Yet the Constitution of 1917, and the revolution that spawned it, would eventually give rise to a series of far-reaching social reforms in Mexico, including the biggest redistribution of land in the history of the Americas and a dramatic expansion of public education. For those reasons, despite its failure to live up to all of its promises, the Mexican Revolution is recognized as the first of the great social revolutions of the twentieth century and one of the most critical events in Mexican history.

Mexico Under Porfirio Díaz

The Mexican Revolution had its roots in the dictatorship of Porfirio Díaz, who ruled Mexico with an iron fist from 1876 to 1911. Remarkably rapid economic growth as well as brutal political oppression marked Díaz's 35-year stranglehold on Mexico. During his long tenure, Mexico acquired more than 10,000 miles (16,000 kilometers) of new railroad track; sugar and other lucrative export crops were produced on vast commercial farms on an unprecedented scale; and oil and mineral production skyrocketed due to a major infusion of foreign money and technological expertise. Yet Mexico's breakneck economic progress under Díaz's autocratic regime benefited only a privileged few. For most of the country's overwhelmingly poor and illiterate population, Díaz's ambitious program of modernization and economic development came at a huge price.

One of seven children, José de la Cruz Porfirio Díaz Mori grew up in humble circumstances. Born in the southern state of Oaxaca in 1830, nine years after Mexico won its independence from Spain, the future dictator was a *mestizo*—a Mexican of mixed Spanish and Indian ancestry. After his father, an innkeeper and part-time blacksmith, died when Porfirio was still a toddler, his widowed mother struggled to feed and educate him and his six siblings.

At his mother's urging, Porfirio enrolled at the age of 13 in a Roman Catholic seminary to prepare for a career as a priest. Four years later, the course of his life was forever changed when he was introduced to Benito Juárez, a respected lawyer and full-blooded Zapotec Indian who had just been elected as Oaxaca's new governor. Inspired by the charismatic governor's example, Porfirio withdrew from the seminary at age 17 and enrolled in law school. He also became active in the Liberal Party, of which Juárez was a leading member. Ever since Mexico had broken free of the Spanish Empire in 1821, the Liberals and their chief opponents, the Conservatives, had competed for control of the country. Composed mainly of modest cattle ranchers and merchants, intellectuals, and rural political leaders, the Liberals stood for federalism (a form of government in which power is shared between a central authority and local political structures), constitutional democracy, and greater separation of church and state. Represented chiefly by hacendados, high-ranking military officials, and the Catholic Church, the Conservatives stood for state religion (Roman Catholicism) and a strong centralized government led by a privileged elite and backed by a powerful professional army.

In 1858, when the long-standing power struggle between Liberals and Conservatives erupted into the War of the Reform, Díaz immediately volunteered to fight for the Liberal side. A natural-born soldier, he played an important part in helping guide the Liberals to victory over their Conservative foes in January 1861. Almost exactly a year later, and just a few months after Juárez, now the Liberal Party leader, was elected as the republic's new president, Mexico was at war again, this time with the French Empire and its imperialistic ruler, Napoleon III. Despite stiff resistance by Liberal-led forces, French troops occupied the capital, Mexico City, by 1864. Napoleon III, supported by prominent Mexican Conservatives, had forced Juárez from office and installed a puppet ruler in the National Palace. Once again, Porfirio Díaz distinguished himself on the battlefield, leading his forces to victory against the French invaders in several well-publicized clashes, including the famous Battle of Puebla on May 5, 1862 (still commemorated by Mexicans as the holiday of Cinco de Mayo). By 1867, when Napoleon III finally decided to pull his troops out of Mexico, Díaz had been promoted to the rank of general and become a national celebrity. The 37-year-old war hero had also developed powerful political ambitions.

DÍAZ'S BUMPY POLITICAL RISE

"Just like his contemporary in the United States, [Civil War] General Ulysses S. Grant," historian Michael Gonzales notes, Díaz sought to "use his military prestige as a springboard into national politics"[1] following the Franco-Mexican War. Yet, to the general's enormous frustration, his political rise was hindered by none other than his old mentor and the man most Mexicans credited with bringing their country through the dark days of the French occupation, President Juárez. After Juárez managed to win an unprecedented fourth term in 1871, an impatient Díaz tried to secure the presidency by force. His rebellion was justified, the general proclaimed, because Juárez had violated Mexico's Constitution, which prohibited presidents from serving two terms in a row. Díaz's main support for the uprising came from his former comrades-in-arms and from local political leaders, who resented Juárez's efforts to strengthen the central government at the expense of the state governments.

Porfirio Díaz, the Mexican general and president, is considered by most historians to be a brutal dictator. The Mexican Revolution ended his long reign, which lasted, except for one brief period, from 1876 to 1911.

On July 18, 1872, as Díaz's rebel army was losing to the president's larger force on the battlefield, Juárez suffered a fatal heart attack. Until new national elections could be arranged, the Mexican Congress appointed the chief justice of the Supreme Court, Sebastián Lerdo de Tejada, as interim president. After generously offering full amnesty to Díaz and his fellow rebels, Lerdo was formally elected president under the Liberal banner in late 1872. Four years later, despite the constitutional prohibition on consecutive presidential terms and the loud objections of Díaz, whose own political ambitions had grown stronger, Lerdo announced that he was running for reelection. After months of quietly building support within the army, as well as between two influential opponents of the Liberal Party that he had once championed—the Catholic Church and the hacendados—Díaz launched an anti-Lerdo rebellion that autumn under the slogan "no reelection."[2] Lerdo had no choice but to resign when Díaz's troops managed to fight their way into Mexico City and occupy the capital. With Lerdo out of the way, Díaz became Mexico's new chief executive in November 1876.

Since he had supposedly taken up arms against Lerdo and Juárez to defend the constitution, Díaz could hardly run for reelection at the end of his first term in 1880. Instead, he endorsed General Manuel González, a loyal supporter in his rebellion against Lerdo. Most historians agree that González was little more than Díaz's puppet, ready and willing to do his bidding in all things, particularly when it came to strengthening the power of the executive branch of the central government. As the end of his term approached, González obligingly declared Díaz the most qualified person to succeed him as president: "I see no other man who possesses the virtues that he does, not only for maintaining peace in the Republic, but also for supporting its institutions."[3]

After Díaz handily won the national election of 1884, it quickly became apparent that he had no intention of relinquishing the presidency again anytime soon. A year before the next presidential election was to take place, conveniently abandoning his earlier commitment to the principle of "no reelection," Díaz persuaded Mexican legislators to amend the constitution to allow for two successive presidential terms. Then, in 1890, he pressured them into passing a second amendment permitting an unlimited number of successive presidential terms by the same individual.

DÍAZ CONSOLIDATES HIS POWER

Díaz's success in securing these constitutional amendments testified not only to his ambition to stay in office indefinitely, but also to his growing domination over Mexican politics. In consolidating his political authority from the late 1870s onward, Díaz relied on a variety of strategies, from election rigging to bribery. By all accounts, the president was a master political manipulator. He skillfully played his rivals against one another, undercut the influence of popular governors by transferring them to cabinet or diplomatic posts, and bought off elected officials at all levels of government, cynically observing that "a dog with a bone in its mouth neither kills nor steals."[4]

At both the national and state level, Díaz replaced officeholders whose loyalty he had even the slightest reason to doubt with personal cronies. Not coincidentally, most of Díaz's gubernatorial and congressional appointees had little or no previous connection with the states or districts they were called on to serve. Appointing outsiders was a smart political move on the president's part, argues historian Gonzales, because it ensured they would be "unencumbered by local family, financial, and political entanglements that might compromise their allegiance to the dictator."[5] Diaz's policy of placing outsiders whom he could more readily control in government posts reached deep into the Mexican countryside, where Díaz appointed hundreds of *jefes políticos*—political bosses—to replace elected village officials.

RULE BY FEAR

Many Mexicans were appalled by Díaz's authoritarian governing style, particularly by his practice of filling state, municipal, and village political offices with nonresidents who were unfamiliar with and, all too often, indifferent to local concerns. Yet few dared to speak out against Díaz or his handpicked appointees. They knew that the president was not above using imprisonment, forced exile, and even murder to silence his critics and enforce his will. As author Frank McLynn observes, Díaz "made it clear that he wanted no opposition, either in presidential elections or elsewhere. Two generals, García de la Cadena and Juan Corona, allowed their names to go forward as presidential hopefuls only to be mysteriously murdered."[6] In 1879, asked by the governor of Veracruz, Luis Mier y Terán, whether he should put nine local men suspected of plotting against Díaz on trial for sedition, the president reportedly ordered Terán to "kill them at once."[7] All of the prisoners were summarily shot.

When Díaz determined that force was necessary to control unruly groups of citizens, whether disgruntled Indians or striking miners, he turned to the federal army and the rural police corps, the *rurales*. Since most Mexicans lived in the countryside during the late nineteenth and early twentieth centuries, the mounted rurales were a critical element of Díaz's disciplinary apparatus. President Juárez had created Mexico's national rural police corps in the early 1860s to fight widespread banditry along the nation's country roads. Under Díaz, the size of this paramilitary force more than doubled, and its members were equipped with the most up-to-date European rifles. Besides patrolling for bandits, the rurales were also used by Díaz to enforce controversial court decisions, break up labor strikes, and squash small-scale peasant uprisings.

At the president's urging, the rurales brutally put down the few popular rebellions that occurred under Díaz's repressive rule before the outbreak of the Mexican Revolution. Rebels "must be punished with the utmost severity," Díaz maintained, "because any leniency shown to them will . . . only encourage them to renewed and constant uprisings."[8] When Indians in the state of Hidalgo rebelled against local authorities for seizing their ancestral lands, for example, the rurales buried the insurgents up to their necks and trampled them to death by riding over them at full gallop. In Sonora, rurales first massacred the entire male population of a Yaqui Indian village after some residents dared to take up arms against a corrupt jefe político and later drowned 200 rebellious Yaquis near the Pacific port of Guaymas.

Along with the rurales, Díaz relied on the Mexican army to strike fear in the hearts of potential insurgents. "There are times," the president once confided to an American reporter, "when a little cannon smoke is not such a bad thing."[9] Resolved to build the federal army into a more professional force, Díaz purchased the latest European weaponry and reformed the national military academy's curriculum to ensure that officers learned the most up-to-date military techniques. Gonzales notes that a stronger army "presented President Díaz with a . . . political dilemma" because, as the former general knew only too well, the Mexican military "had produced the vast majority of [the republic's] presidents, usually via coups d'état."[10] Consequently, during his decades-long rule, the president slashed the size of the army from 30,000 to 14,000 troops and the number of generals by 25 percent. To hinder ambitious officers from developing an independent power base, he also made a point of regularly rotating generals and regimental commanders from one military zone to another within the country.

BUILDING MEXICO'S ECONOMY WITH FOREIGN MONEY

Díaz justified his brutal authoritarianism on the grounds that political stability was essential to the development of Mexico's economy. Indeed, there can be no question that decades of political upheaval and warfare had severely stunted the republic's economic growth during much of the nineteenth century. In the 55 years between Mexican independence and Díaz's first term in office, the presidency had changed hands more than six dozen times. Díaz argued that political uncertainty along with widespread banditry in the countryside had scared off the foreign investors and technological experts Mexico needed to modernize and expand its transportation network, effectively exploit its rich natural resources, and create a strong industrial base.

One of Díaz's first economic priorities on assuming power was to enlarge the country's woefully inadequate railroad system. In the late 1870s, Mexico had just over 400 miles (645 km) of rail track as compared with 90,000 miles (144,800 km) of track in the United States. Yet the republic's rugged geography, Díaz realized, meant that a well-developed rail transportation network was essential to economic progress. Three major wars during the previous three decades—the Mexican-American War of 1846–1848, the War of the Reform, and the Franco-Mexican War—combined with chronic political instability had left the Mexican economy in a shambles and venture capital in short supply. Consequently, the president quickly decided that financing the construction of Mexico's costly new rail system was going to require a major infusion of capital from outside of the country. To encourage U.S. and other foreign railroad contractors, Díaz promised them large land grants paralleling the tracks, tax exemptions, and wage caps for local laborers. Historian Adolfo Gilly notes that railroad companies, particularly in the United States, responded enthusiastically to the president's generous offers and "the country's railway network grew at dizzying speed."[11] By 1910, Mexico's overall railroad track had increased thirty-fold to nearly 12,000 miles (19,300 km).

As Mexico's railroad system grew, so did its largely undeveloped mining and oil industries. Now that goods could be shipped more efficiently and cheaply than ever before, oil, one of the country's most plentiful natural resources, and valuable minerals such as silver, copper, and lead could be transported in bulk to refineries in northern Mexico or across the border in the United States. Like most of the capital used to construct Mexico's railroad system, much of the funds used to drill oil wells and sink mine shafts came from outside the country, chiefly the United States and Great Britain. Enticed by tax breaks and a variety of other attractive incentives, American investors alone came to own more than 50 percent of Mexico's oil fields and 75 percent of its mines. U.S. corporations, along with British, French, and German companies, also founded iron and steelworks, textile mills, and cement factories in Mexico.

DÍAZ'S PRO-HACENDADO LAND POLICIES

Among the many lucrative deals that the Díaz regime offered to foreign investors was the opportunity to buy public lands in Mexico at bargain-basement prices. Many of them, especially Americans, were only too happy to take advantage of the president's generosity. Nonetheless, during the Díaz era the vast majority of the republic's land was not held by foreigners but rather by an elite group of wealthy Mexican hacendados. When Díaz assumed power in 1876, a sizable portion of the nation's best farming and grazing land was already owned by several hundred ultra-rich hacendado families. Under his long rule, however, the concentration of Mexico's agricultural land in the hands of a relatively small number of very large landholders increased dramatically.

The transfer of more and more of Mexico's territory to a wealthy few during Díaz's presidency was directly linked to a controversial law he pushed through Congress in 1883. Designed to encourage large-scale commercial farming, the law authorized private companies or individuals to survey— determine the precise boundaries of—the country's millions of acres of public land. As compensation for their time, surveyors were granted one-third of the lands they measured and an opportunity to purchase the remaining two-thirds at rock-bottom prices. According to Gonzales, since "most surveyors were also local hacendados," this arrangement proved an enormous boon to well-off landowners looking to supplement their already substantial holdings.[12]

During the 1880s, *ejidos*—communal properties traditionally held by Indian villages throughout Mexico—also increasingly fell under the control of local hacendados. The Mexican government had begun to permit nonnatives to take over some of these properties in the mid-1800s. Under Díaz, however, the number and magnitude of the communal land grabs grew sharply as his regime consistently took the side of wealthy landowners over poor villagers. By the early 1900s, most rural Mexican villages had been stripped of their ejidos, which now totaled barely 2 percent of the republic's overall acreage, down from 25 percent when Díaz first took office.

UNPRECEDENTED PROSPERITY AND POVERTY

Díaz's pro-hacendado land policies—combined with his dramatic expansion of the country's rail transportation system—proved a tremendous boon to commercial agriculture in Mexico. Huge cattle ranches soon appeared in Sonora and other northern states, while vast haciendas devoted to lucrative export crops such as rubber, sugar, cotton, and henequen (a plant whose coarse fiber was used in making rope), emerged in the southern states. By 1900, bolstered by the country's booming agricultural, mineral, and oil production, Mexico's foreign trade had increased 300 percent in the years since Díaz first came to power. Yet historians estimate that the striking growth in Mexico's economy under his dictatorship benefited no more than 10 percent of the country's nearly 14 million inhabitants. Thomas Skidmore and Peter Smith note, "While the wealthy prospered and duly copied the ways of the European aristocracy, the vast majority of Mexicans faced grinding poverty."[13]

After being stripped of their communal land, most small-scale farmers and herders were compelled to toil for starvation

In the years before the Mexican Revolution, the poor were brutally exploited, particularly in rural areas. In this engraving, Mexican political cartoonist Jose Guadalupe Posada depicts the cruel treatment of peasants by hacienda owners and their overseers.

wages on nearby haciendas just to provide the basic necessities for themselves and their families. The almost total disappearance of ejidos during Díaz's rule created a large surplus of unskilled labor in the Mexican countryside, meaning that profit-hungry hacendados had little incentive to raise their field hands' wages. While the average agricultural worker's wages stagnated, food prices soared as more and more of Mexico's arable land was devoted to export crops and less and less to corn—the basic staple of the peasant diet. Some hacienda workers did not even receive any cash wages. Instead, they were compensated for their backbreaking labor in certificates that could only be redeemed at a general store owned by the hacendado. Since prices at the general stores were typically inflated, thousands of agricultural laborers ended up in a state of perpetual debt. This turned them into virtual slaves of their employers because, according to Mexican law, any laborer who owed money to a hacendado had to remain on his land until the debt had been paid off in full.

Although most of the numerous mines and factories that opened in Mexico during Díaz's régime proved to be lucrative investments for their chiefly foreign owners, the Mexicans who toiled in them were scarcely better off than the country's exploited rural masses. Mining and industrial workers slaved from sunrise to sunset, six days a week, for pay that, while higher than the wages offered on most haciendas, was still barely above subsistence level. Copper miners in Sonora and textile workers in Veracruz tried to force their employers into raising wages by going on strike in late 1906 and early 1907. In both cases, however, the strikes were quickly halted after the government came out in support of the mine and mill owners. In Veracruz, Díaz even went as far as to use federal troops to break the strike. Hundreds of workers were killed or wounded by the heavily armed soldiers, sending an unmistakable message to disgruntled laborers all over Mexico.

Mexico's workforce was effectively cowed by the government's ruthless show of force in Veracruz, just as the president had intended. Thus, despite growing popular dissatisfaction with Díaz's oppressive policies and the widening gap between the country's poor masses and wealthy few, there was no nationwide call for revolution. It would take a major international economic downturn, combined with some highly uncharacteristic political bungling on Díaz's part, before the Mexican people were finally prepared to take up arms against his tyrannical regime.

The Revolution Begins

Mexico's economy grew at an impressive pace as a result of Porfirio Díaz's strongly pro-big business and pro-hacendado policies. Nonetheless, only a small elite group of Mexicans benefited from this economic boom. Yet even they could not escape the effects of an international recession, triggered in late 1907 by a crisis on Wall Street. The massive economic downturn did not bode well for the aging and increasingly unpopular Díaz. It meant that, should the president face a serious challenge to his authoritarian rule at home, "fewer and fewer hands would be raised to save him," historian Frank McLynn writes.[1] In 1910, after the 80-year-old dictator rigged yet another presidential election to secure his eighth term in office, that is exactly what happened.

The international economic crisis that began with the Wall Street crash of 1907 had repercussions in every sector of the Mexican economy. Plummeting silver prices and declining demand for copper and other precious metals by Mexico's chief trading partner, the United States, took a toll on the once-flourishing mining industry. Unfavorable market conditions in the United States and Europe also battered northern Mexico's other key export industries, including textiles, timber, and cattle ranching, and unemployed workers flocked to the region's towns in search of jobs. In the southern state of Morelos, a new high tariff on imported sugar in the United States, designed to protect its domestic agriculture, hurt sugar plantation and mill owners and their employees alike. Thousands of laid-off agricultural and mill workers—many formerly self-sufficient farmers whose villages' communal fields had been confiscated under Díaz's pro-hacendado land policies—crowded Ayala and other towns in Morelos in search of work.

In 1908 and 1909, droughts and crop failures across much of the country's northern half worsened an already difficult situation. The poor corn harvests that plagued the republic during those years were particularly devastating, since corn was the basic stable of the national diet. To stave off famine, the country was forced to import corn from the United States at inflated prices. Nonetheless, chronic food shortfalls devolved into full-fledged famine in some rural communities. Although Mexico's huge lower class was most affected by the high corn prices, as the country's economy floundered, all but the very wealthiest Mexicans felt the pinch of escalating food costs.

Díaz's response to Mexico's economic woes, including the skyrocketing price of corn, did nothing to endear the aging dictator to his countrymen. Seemingly indifferent to the plight of ordinary Mexicans, the president and his top economic advisers in Mexico City opposed any governmental interference in what they viewed as the natural workings of the marketplace. Consequently, the regime refused to provide financial assistance either to hungry peasants and unemployed workers or to the business owners who suffered crushing losses as a result of the international economic downturn. During the rapid economic expansion that characterized the first three decades of his rule, only a relatively small number of courageous souls near the bottom of the economic ladder—such as Sonora's rebellious Yaquis or the striking textile workers of Veracruz— dared to challenge Díaz's authoritarian policies. As the national economy soured, however, growing numbers of middle- and upper-class Mexicans began to clamor for more political influence, driving the autocratic president to commit what would turn out to be a profound political blunder.

"I SHALL NOT SERVE AGAIN"

In February 1908, Díaz granted a long interview to American reporter James Creelman, "which was largely a self-serving puff for his achievements, real and alleged," McLynn observes.[2] When Creelman pressed him regarding his undemocratic policies, Díaz, eager to strike a statesmanlike pose, committed what historians agree was the mistake that directly contributed to his downfall just two years later. Díaz had always maintained that he had only adopted authoritarian methods to bring desperately needed stability to Mexico following decades of political upheaval. Now, after more than 30 years under his firm guidance, Díaz proclaimed that his homeland was at last ready to advance toward a full-fledged democracy, nobly assuring Creelman that he would "welcome an opposition party in the Mexican Republic."[3] Then, as evidence of his seriousness, Díaz dropped an even bigger bombshell regarding the next presidential election, scheduled for mid-1910. "Whatever the opinions of my friends and supporters," he avowed, "I shall stand down from power at the end of the current term of office, and I shall not serve again."[4]

Díaz's unexpected declaration that he would not run for reelection or try to prevent the rebirth of a political party system in Mexico created an immediate sensation. Although from the very start "Díaz's inner circle did not believe him," historian Michael Gonzales contends:

> [M]any Mexicans took Díaz seriously. They began organizing political clubs, writing party platforms critical of the regime, and announcing their candidacies for local, state, and national offices. This spontaneous outburst of enthusiasm at the prospects for free elections must have distressed Díaz and his inner circle, who had lost touch with popular political sentiment. The country was clearly ready for a change.[5]

That Díaz was so out of touch with the pulse of the nation in 1908 that he failed to foresee the enormous impact his phony political largesse would have on the voting public was hardly surprising. By this time, the president's carefully crafted system of political control was beginning to fray at the edges. In the countryside, Frank McLynn observes, the dictator's local political bosses

> had become complacent and filed reassuring reports to Díaz, containing only what he wanted to hear. His network of spies and agents became impossibly swollen in size, full of corrupt and time-serving drones who regarded "intelligence" as a sinecure [a position that requires little work but furnishes a salary]. . . . Most corrupt and incompetent of all Díaz's agents, however, were the *rurales*. . . . Supposed to sniff out all opposition to don Porfirio, they utterly failed to do so, largely because they were too busy handing worthless sons and nephews into sinecures, padding payrolls, and arranging for kickbacks, sweeteners and payola from protection rackets.[6]

With the foundations of both his repressive rule and the national economy weaker than they had ever been since he took office, Díaz could hardly have chosen a less auspicious time to make political promises that he had no intention of fulfilling. When, to the dictator's dismay, a strong opposition candidate for the presidency emerged the following year, his political fate had already been sealed.

BERNARDO REYES AND THE PARTIDO DEMOCRÁTICO

By the end of 1908, it was evident that, despite what he said during his interview with Creelman, the president planned to run for reelection in 1910. With the presidency now seemingly beyond its grasp, Mexico's leading new political party, the Partido Nacionalista Democrático (Nationalist Democratic Party), tried to make General Bernardo Reyes, the well-liked governor of Nuevo León, the dictator's vice president. Díaz, who had only agreed to allow the creation of the post of vice president a few years earlier, had other ideas, however.

Most Mexicans—including Díaz himself—assumed that whoever held the vice presidency when the aged dictator finally got around to retiring would be his successor. Apparently determined that his successor should not outshine him, Díaz placed the notoriously corrupt governor of Sonora, Ramón Corral, in the post in 1904. Five years later, when General Reyes began to receive positive attention from the press and voting public as a contender for the vice presidency, Díaz made it clear that he intended to keep Corral on the ticket in the upcoming election. Then, just to be on the safe side, the president ordered Reyes to leave the country on a lengthy diplomatic mission to Europe. After publicly endorsing Corral as Díaz's running mate, Reyes meekly headed across the Atlantic. Whether the general's behavior was rooted in loyalty to Díaz or fear of what might happen to him if he dared disobey the autocratic president remains a matter of speculation among historians.

Díaz's obvious relief at Reyes's departure, however, was to prove premature. By the time the general sailed for Europe in November 1909, Díaz's campaign to maintain his long stranglehold over Mexican politics faced a far more serious challenge than Reyes's halfhearted pursuit of the vice presidency. And it came from a most unexpected quarter.

AN UNLIKELY REVOLUTIONARY

Historian McLynn writes that the man destined to bring down the Díaz regime, Francisco Ignacio Madero González, "was surely the most unlikely revolutionary of all time."[7] Born into one of the 10 wealthiest families in Mexico, Madero was barely five feet (152 centimeters) tall with a slight build and a quavering, high-pitched voice. Widely considered as eccentric, he was a strict vegetarian and an avid follower of spiritualism, a religious movement that taught that the living can communicate with the spirits of the dead. To the enormous embarrassment of his prominent family, Madero insisted that he received regular messages from the deceased, including his brother, Raúl, who had died as a young child, and such famous historical figures as Benito Juárez and President John Adams of the United States.

Madero was a complex man. While some who did not know him well were quick to dismiss him as "an impractical, dreamy-eyed mystic" because of his peculiar religious beliefs, Eileen Welsome writes, "in reality he was an enterprising and resourceful businessman who before the age of thirty had acquired a fortune that was independent of his family's great wealth."[8] After studying economics in Paris and agriculture at the University of California in Berkeley, he returned home in 1893 to assume the management of several family properties, including a large cotton plantation in northeastern Mexico. He was just 20 years old. Under his adroit supervision, the cotton plantation prospered. He then used some of his profits to build an ice factory, soap factory, and meteorological observatory on the plantation grounds. Unusually enlightened by the standards of most hacendados in his treatment of his workers, Madero provided his employees with generous wages, comfortable housing, and free medical care.

By the time Díaz held his interview with Creelman in early 1908, Madero had become deeply concerned about Mexico's growing economic troubles and rising social tensions, which he feared could leave the country vulnerable to foreign invasion. At the root of Mexico's problems, he believed, was the corrupt and undemocratic political system Díaz had created to maintain his personal power. In early 1909, hoping to stir the Mexican electorate into demanding political reform, Madero published a book on the upcoming presidential election, *The Presidential Succession in 1910*. In it, he blasted the harmful influence that one-man rule had had on Mexico and called for free and open elections, single presidential terms, and the right of the Mexican people to choose their own vice president at the polls.

THE PRESIDENTIAL ELECTION OF 1910

The Presidential Succession turned the previously unknown Madero into a national celebrity. Middle- and upper-class Mexicans who disapproved of Díaz's autocratic practices were particularly drawn to Madero's book because it called for democratic political reforms without demanding economic or social reforms that might threaten their own wealth or positions. Encouraged by the positive response to his book, Madero decided in mid-1909 to invest a big chunk of his vast personal fortune into a national campaign to promote democratic principles in Mexico. As head of the newly formed Anti-Re-Electionist Party, Madero embarked on a long speaking tour of Mexico in June 1909. At every stop he made, he urged his audiences to unite behind the cause of democratic political reform. Heartened by the large numbers of Mexicans who flocked to hear him, Madero resolved to challenge Díaz for the presidency.

During the first few months of Madero's candidacy, Díaz convinced himself that the slightly built hacendado with a reputation for eccentricity posed no real threat to his power.

Francisco Madero was an unusual revolutionary. A spiritualist and a member of the upper class, he became the center around which opposition to the dictatorship of Porfirio Díaz united. Once Díaz was overthrown, however, control over the revolution quickly slipped from Madero's grasp.

Even after the Anti-Re-Electionist Party officially nominated Madero for president in April 1910 under the slogan, "a real vote and no boss rule," Díaz remained unfazed.[9] By mid-May, with the national elections just two months away and Madero's rallies drawing huge crowds, the president was finally becoming alarmed. On June 14, a worried Díaz had Madero and hundreds of his Anti-Re-Electionist colleagues arrested and jailed on trumped-up charges of sedition. Three weeks later, Díaz "won" the presidential election by a landslide. On October 4, Congress obligingly certified the results of the blatantly rigged election, in which Madero had supposedly received just 183 votes. The following day, in response to the repeated pleas of Madero's prominent family, Díaz agreed to free him in exchange for his pledge to remain in the country. As soon as he was released, Madero fled across the U.S. border, arriving in San Antonio, Texas, on October 7. Once again, Díaz had seriously underestimated his opponent.

THE PLAN OF SAN LUIS POTOSÍ

A confirmed pacifist, Madero had always opposed using violence to end Díaz's long dictatorship. But after his arrest and imprisonment, Madero concluded that the only way to pry Díaz out of office was through an armed rebellion. Consequently, after reaching San Antonio, Madero began to work on a revolutionary manifesto. He dubbed it the "Plan of San Luis Potosí," in honor of the city in northern Mexico where he had been held before escaping across the U.S. border.

Issued in mid-October, the plan declared the election of 1910 null and void. Until a new national election could be arranged, the manifesto called for Madero himself to act as the republic's provisional president. Madero's revolutionary blueprint also demanded an independent judicial system, a genuinely free press, and an end to the reelection of presidents. Although social and economic issues were barely mentioned in the document, Madero did urge the return of some confiscated lands to Indian villages, perhaps in hopes of winning popular support for his rebellion. Madero closed his plan with a daring call to battle: "I have designated Sunday, the 20th of next November, for all the towns in the Republic to rise in arms after 6 o'clock P.M."[10]

All in all, Madero's revolutionary program promised little to the nation's downtrodden masses. Yet, as historians Michael C. Meyer, William L. Sherman, and Susan M. Deeds note, "the boldness of the statement and the self-confidence it reflected struck a responsive chord" among poor as well as better-off Mexicans.[11] Despite the plan's nearly exclusive focus on political reform, many lower-class Mexicans, inspired by the hope that Madero, once in power, would initiate social reforms aimed at lessening the chasm between Mexico's haves and have-nots, joined Anti-Re-Electionist leaders throughout the country in preparing for rebellion.

¡VIVA LA REVOLUCIÓN!

On the night of November 19, Madero slipped back across the border into Mexico. Two hundred armed rebels under the command of his uncle were supposed to meet him near the Texas border. To Madero's consternation, however, there was a miscommunication and the rendezvous never took place. Consequently, although November 20, 1910, is officially considered as the starting date of the Mexican Revolution, no military action of any note actually occurred on that day. When the expected rebel force failed to show up, Madero hastily made his way back to San Antonio. Whatever doubts he may have harbored on November 20 regarding the true extent of the Mexican people's commitment to ousting Díaz would soon be laid to rest, however.

Scattered bands of guerrilla fighters—rallying to the cry of "¡Viva la Revolución!" ("Long live the revolution!") over the next several months—kept Madero's rebellion alive by raiding federal outposts, dynamiting railroad tracks, and attacking local government officials and hacendados. In the south-central state of Morelos, whose overwhelmingly poor and rural population had lost hundreds of thousands of acres of farmland to big sugar planters as a result of Díaz's pro-hacendado policies, a peasant army commanded by the charismatic land reformer Emiliano Zapata stormed local haciendas and clashed with federal troops. But the largest and most effective of the

PANCHO VILLA

Pancho Villa, or Doroteo Arango as his sharecropper parents originally named him, was born on a large hacienda in the northern state of Durango on June 6, 1878. Details of Doroteo's early life are sketchy. According to Villa's published memoirs, when he was 16, he shot and wounded the owner of the hacienda where his family lived after the hacendado tried to rape his sister. Escaping into the nearby mountains, young Doroteo soon joined a gang of bandits and cattle rustlers. After eluding the authorities for seven years, he was apprehended in 1901 on charges of robbery and assault and sentenced to serve one year in the federal army. He soon deserted and fled to the state of Chihuahua, which borders Durango on the northeast. Assuming the alias of Francisco Villa (Pancho is a common nickname for Francisco), he worked as a mule driver, butcher, and miner in Chihuahua, while carrying out the occasional robbery on the side.

Historians have long speculated about Villa's motives in responding to Madero's call to revolution in November 1910. After recruiting a 700-man army composed of Chihuahuan cowboys, unemployed mine workers, and poor farmers, Villa himself claimed that he was drawn to Madero's cause by a desire to help Mexico's exploited masses. A flamboyant and controversial figure, Villa has had his share of critics over the

various rebel armies in the struggle to topple Díaz was centered in the mineral-rich northern state of Chihuahua and commanded by Pascual Orozco, ably assisted by the man destined to become the revolution's most famous military leader, the dashing Francisco "Pancho" Villa.

Born into a lower middle-class family in western Chihuahua in 1882, Pascual Orozco was determined to move up in the

years, some of whom have suggested that his revolutionary activities were spurred not by a genuine concern for Mexico's oppressed masses, but rather by the promise of plunder. Yet despite Villa's criminal background, there is "no evidence he joined the Madero revolution for purposes of looting, pillage, and banditry," Villa's biographer, Friedrich Katz, contends. "On the contrary," Katz writes, Villa's "troops were considered among the most disciplined in the revolutionary army, and there is no evidence that he acquired any significant wealth . . . during that period of his life."*

Renowned for his courage under fire as well as his superb marksmanship and riding skills, Villa inspired enormous devotion from his soldiers. On "the battlefield, amid the dust and smoke," Eileen Welsome writes, "his galloping figure would so inspire his men that they would hurl themselves willingly into the withering machine-gun fire of their enemies."** A century after the Mexican Revolution erupted, many Mexicans still view the bandit turned rebel general as one of the revolution's most appealing and charismatic heroes.

* Friedrich Katz, *The Life and Times of Pancho Villa*. Palo Alto, Calif.: Stanford University Press, 1998, p. 805.

** Eileen Welsome, *The General and the Jaguar: Pershing's Hunt for Pancho Villa*. New York: Little, Brown and Company, 2006, p. 22.

A circa March 1913 photo of General Pascual Orozco *(center with dark hat and mustache)* and his officers and men. His forces scored a major victory over Diaz's troops early in the revolution.

world from his earliest days. After spending much of his youth toiling as a mule driver, he managed to save enough money to purchase a small gold mine. By 1910, the year the revolution began, Orozco was making a comfortable living from his mine and other commercial investments. Yet he deeply resented the fact that a tiny handful of wealthy families and jefes políticos with ties to Díaz dominated his home state's economic and political life. Consequently, when Madero issued his Plan of San Luis Potosí, Orozco immediately began to assemble a diverse army of Chihuahuan cowboys, miners, shopkeepers, and hacienda workers to help bring down Díaz's regime. During the revolution's first weeks, Orozco and his commandos won several well-publicized victories against federal forces

in western Chihuahua. Impressed by Orozco's battlefield suc-
cesses, other Chihuahuan revolutionary leaders, most notably
Pancho Villa, soon placed themselves and their armies under
Orozco's command.

In January 1911, with revolutionary violence spreading
throughout much of the country, Orozco and his troops scored
a major triumph against Díaz's forces when they ambushed and
all but annihilated a big federal convoy in Cañon de Mal Paso,
Chihuahua. Greatly encouraged by this development, Madero
decided to return to his homeland. On February 14, he crossed
the Texas-Mexico border near Ciudad Juárez, a major commercial center in northern Chihuahua on the Rio Grande, to take
charge of the revolutionary forces fighting in his name.

THE FALL OF DÍAZ

During the winter and early spring of 1911, rebel forces gained
significant ground against federal troops not only in Chihuahua, but throughout much of the Mexican countryside and in a
number of key cities as well. The federal army, commanded by
aged generals and composed mainly of conscripts, lacked the
leadership, discipline, and "sheer numbers to handle a large-
scale uprising on several fronts," historians Michael Meyer
and William Beezley observe.[12] In April, Orozco and his top
general, Villa, persuaded Madero that their battle-seasoned
revolutionary armies were ready to wrest the critical port city
and railway hub of Ciudad Juárez from Díaz's poorly led and
demoralized forces.

By early May, Orozco, Villa, Madero, and a large rebel
army had gathered on the outskirts of Ciudad Juárez, poised to
attack the city's federal garrison. At the last minute, however,
Madero suddenly lost his nerve and ordered a retreat. Juárez's
location directly across the Rio Grande from El Paso, Texas,
worried him. Should any rebel shells stray off course and hit
El Paso, Madero feared, the U.S. government was almost sure
to retaliate. Disgusted by what he viewed as Madero's excessive

A photograph of the famous Mexican revolutionary leader Francisco "Pancho" Villa, circa 1914. A modern-day Robin Hood, Villa and his supporters seized hacienda lands and gave them to peasants and soldiers.

caution, Orozco defied his commander's order, launching a fierce assault on the Ciudad Juárez garrison on May 8. On May 10, with his troops dangerously low on ammunition and cut off from all sources of fresh water, the federal fort's commander raised the white flag of surrender.

Barely more than a week after their triumph at Ciudad Juárez, the rebels won another important victory when Emiliano Zapata and his peasant army in Morelos captured the heavily defended city of Cuautla. In the wake of the victories in Chihuahua and Morelos, the revolution gained momentum throughout the republic. One state after another fell under rebel control. Finally ready to acknowledge that his long dictatorship had come to an end, Díaz sent negotiators to Ciudad Juárez, where Madero had established a provisional government, to work out a peaceful transfer of power. The resulting Treaty of Ciudad Juárez stipulated that the president and his vice president resign by the last day of the month and that Díaz's secretary of foreign relations, Francisco León de la Barra, would serve as interim president until new general elections could be arranged.

On May 25, 1911, Díaz formally submitted his resignation to the Mexican Congress. A few days later he set sail from Veracruz for exile in Paris, where he died not quite four years later at the age of 84. Edward Bell, an American newspaper editor living in Mexico City, described the public's ecstatic response to the first reports of Díaz's resignation: "Within an hour the news had traveled to the furthest corner of the capital. . . . all was joy. By eight o'clock that night a monster parade wound through the capital streets. . . . Cheers for Madero rent the heavens. The revolution had won."[13] Yet, while the Mexican people were finally free of the despotic Díaz, it would soon become clear that the revolution was far from over.

Madero
Takes Charge

"Madero has unleashed a tiger. Now let's see if he can control it," Porfirio Díaz sarcastically remarked as he left Mexico for exile in France in May 1911.[1] Díaz's doubts regarding Madero's ability to control the revolution he had launched six months earlier turned out to be well founded. From the beginning of his presidency, Madero struggled to rein in the land-hungry peasants and struggling workers with whom he had formed a shaky coalition to unseat the hated dictator. Most Mexicans who rose up against Díaz viewed the revolution's chief aims very differently from Madero, the new president quickly discovered. While Madero merely envisioned a more democratic national government, they wanted a more egalitarian social and economic order as well. By the first anniversary of his inauguration, Madero's reluctance to go beyond moderate political changes to enact sweeping social and economic reforms had left thousands of his onetime supporters bitter and defiant.

In October 1911, Madero won the popular vote by a landslide in the first truly democratic presidential elections in Mexico in three and a half decades. Even so, by the time the elections were held, some rebel leaders, including the celebrated general and reformer Emiliano Zapata, had already developed serious misgivings about Madero's willingness to effect meaningful change. Concerns among the revolutionaries regarding the true extent of Madero's commitment to land redistribution and other progressive social reforms had begun the previous May with his appointment of Francisco León de la Barra, a former member of Díaz's cabinet, as interim president. When de la Barra filled most of the positions in his cabinet with other associates of the fallen dictator, there were ominous rumblings within the revolutionary ranks. Madero, however, appeared oblivious to the growing discontent among the very men who had put him in power.

From the start of his anti-Díaz rebellion, Madero had emphasized that he wanted to effect political, not social, change in Mexico. Nonetheless, the peasants and workers who risked their lives on the battlefield to oust Díaz believed that Madero, once in office, would reward their sacrifice by championing their interests over those of the country's privileged few. After formally assuming the presidency on November 6, 1911, however, Madero excluded populist heroes and social reformers like Zapata from key political positions at the national and local levels. Instead, Madero awarded influential government posts to fellow members of Mexico's upper and middle classes, most of whom had contributed little or nothing to the overthrow of Díaz. Following in de la Barra's footsteps, Madero appointed more social conservatives, including several members of his own wealthy and prominent family, than liberals to his cabinet. Michael Gonzales writes: "Together, the conservatives would block any initiative put forward by more progressive cabinet ministers, several of whom resigned after a few months in office."[2]

As he had promised to do in his Plan of San Luis Potosí, President Madero immediately turned his attention to what was the single most important issue for most of the revolution's lower-class supporters: agrarian reform. But Mexico's peasantry and their leadership were deeply disappointed by the meager changes to the current system of land distribution that the Madero government was prepared to make. The Madero administration agreed to purchase 25 million acres (10 million hectares) of the huge public tracts that had fallen under private ownership during Díaz's regime and resell the land to any Mexican citizens who desired it. Yet growing concern with keeping the national debt under control meant that the government allocated just 10 million pesos to its land redistribution program. The federal government was able to purchase far fewer acres than originally promised, and much of the land the government did buy was of low quality—too rocky or infertile to be farmed successfully. To add insult to injury, those Mexicans who most needed the land could not afford even the low-interest mortgages offered by the government. In the end, the best and largest of the tracts were bought up by a handful of wealthy Mexican and American investors with ties to the old Díaz regime.

The second plank of Madero's land reform program—a pledge to enforce all court decisions concerning disputed seizures of communal lands—also offered little to Mexico's poorest citizens since only "a handful of cases were settled in favor of the villages," historians Michael Meyer, William Sherman, and Susan Deeds write. The burden of proof inevitably lay with the dispossessed villagers rather than the lands' current owners, and "few village leaders were able to cope with the bewildering legal arguments thrown in their faces by the hacendados' lawyers," the authors observe.[3] Nor did it help that most Indian communities held their ejidos through customary right and lacked formal written titles to the land.

In the area of labor reform, the Madero administration also made few concessions to Mexico's lower class. In 1912, Madero authorized the creation of a Department of Labor, the first in Mexican history. Yet the new department was allotted a budget of just 46,000 pesos, and its head, Rafael Hernández, Madero's conservative minister of public development, almost invariably favored factory and mine owners over workers. In sharp contrast to Díaz, Madero permitted workers to organize openly into labor unions. Nonetheless, determined to do all he could to protect the nation's still fragile economy, Madero used armed police units and federal troops to suppress strikes on a number of occasions, turning large segments of Mexico's working class against him in the process.

ZAPATA AND AGRARIAN REFORM

The first major revolutionary leader to renounce the Madero regime was Emiliano Zapata, who was incensed by the new president's hesitancy to enact meaningful agrarian reform. Born in 1879 in the village of Anenecuilco in northeastern Morelos, Zapata was of mixed Indian and Spanish heritage. By the standards of rural Morelos, the Zapatas were not poor. Emiliano's father owned a small plot of land and some livestock, and the family lived in a solid stone and adobe house instead of a simple hut. After both of Emiliano's parents died when he was still a teenager, young Zapata farmed the few acres of land they left to him, supplementing his income by working as a horse trainer and mule driver.

By the time he was in his late twenties, Zapata, although far from wealthy, had become one of the most respected men in Anenecuilco. He was admired not only for his exceptional

During the Mexican Revolution, Emiliano Zapata formed and commanded an important revolutionary force. Widely renowned as a central voice of the revolution, he was the first revolutionary leader to break with the Madero government.

horse riding and training skills, but also for his outspoken support for his fellow villagers against the big sugar planters who had taken advantage of Díaz's pro-hacendado policies to seize most of Anenecuilco's communal lands. In 1909, the villagers unanimously elected Zapata as chief of the Anenecuilco council, making him responsible for defending the community's interests before the state and national governments.

Zapata traveled to Mexico City to discuss with Madero the return of traditional lands to his village and other dispossessed Morelos communities. The meeting between the two leaders was fraught with drama. After Madero refused to consider Zapata's request that he restore confiscated village properties to their original owners at once, insisting instead that all land disputes involving native communities and hacendados must be decided in the courts, Zapata approached Madero's desk, his rifle in his hand. Pointing at Madero's gold watch, he asked, "If I take advantage of the fact that I'm armed and take away your watch and keep it, and after a while we meet, both of us armed the same, would you have a right to demand that I give it back?" Of course, Madero replied. "Well," concluded Zapata, "that's exactly what has happened to us in Morelos, where a few planters have taken over by force the villages' lands. My soldiers—the armed farmers and all the people in the villages— demand that I tell you, with full respect, that they want the restitution of their lands to get underway right now."[4]

THE PLAN OF AYALA

Although Madero continued to insist that all questions regarding the ownership of former ejidos be settled in the courts, a frustrated Zapata adopted a wait-and-see approach toward the new regime. When interim president de la Barra ordered all revolutionary commando units to disband during the summer of 1911, however, Zapata dragged his heels. In August, an impatient de la Barra ordered federal troops under the command of one of Díaz's most ruthless former generals,

Victoriano Huerta, to enforce the demobilization order, by whatever means necessary. Madero was appalled when he learned that Huerta's troops had opened fire on a band of Zapatistas—the popular name for Zapata's followers—near Cuernavaca, Morelos. Yet, fairly or not, after the incident at Cuernavaca, Zapata lost all faith not only in de la Barra but also in Madero. Accompanied by his commandos, Zapata withdrew into the mountains of Puebla, east of Morelos. Drawn to the Zapatistas' motto of *"Tierra y Libertad"* ("Land and Liberty") disgruntled peasants from neighboring regions flocked to the rebel leader's cause.

THE PLAN OF AYALA

Written by Emiliano Zapata with the assistance of a local Morelos schoolteacher, the Plan of Ayala opened by attacking President Madero for betraying "the faith, the cause, the justice, and the liberties of the people," before spelling out Zapata's radical land reform program. Excerpts from the famous revolutionary document appear below:

6. . . . [We] give notice that [regarding] the fields, timber, and water which the landlords . . . or bosses have usurped, the pueblos or citizens who have the titles corresponding to those properties will immediately enter into possession of that real estate of which they have been despoiled by the bad faith of our oppressors. . . .

7. In virtue of the fact that the immense majority of Mexican . . . citizens are owners of no more than the land they walk on, suffering the horrors of poverty

After Madero officially assumed the presidency in early November 1911, Zapata decided the time had come to turn his crusade against the government's agrarian policies from a regional rebellion into a national revolt. On November 25, Zapata issued the Plan of Ayala, demanding Madero's overthrow and the immediate return of communal lands to villages throughout the country. The plan also called upon a man whose military assistance Zapata was especially eager to obtain, the talented Chihuahuan rebel general Pascual Orozco, to command the new revolutionary campaign. Armed conflict between Zapatistas and federal troops erupted immediately

without being able to improve their social condition in any way . . . , because lands, timber, and water are monopolized in a few hands, for this cause there will be expropriated the third part of those monopolies from the powerful proprietors of them . . . in order that . . . the Mexicans' . . . well-being may improve in all and for all. . . .

15. Mexicans: consider that the . . . bad faith of one man is shedding blood in a scandalous manner, because he is incapable of governing; consider that his system of government is . . . trampling with the brute force of bayonets on our institutions; and thus, as we raised up our weapons to elevate him to power, we again raise them up against him for defaulting on his promises to the Mexican people and for having betrayed the revolution initiated by him, we are not personalists, we are partisans of principles and not of men!*

*Quoted in John Womack Jr., *Zapata and the Mexican Revolution.* New York: Vintage Books, 1968, pp. 401-404.

after the plan's publication and spread rapidly from Puebla and Morelos to nearby states in south-central Mexico. Although Orozco declined Zapata's offer to oversee his new insurrection, Zapatista forces controlled much of the Morelos countryside, along with a number of towns and haciendas throughout south-central Mexico, by early 1912.

A SERIES OF REVOLTS IN THE NORTH

From late 1911 to early 1912, the Madero government was forced to put down a series of rebellions in northern Mexico, making it all the more difficult to gain control over the expanding crisis to the south of Mexico City. In mid-December 1911, General Bernardo Reyes, Díaz's onetime ally, who had returned to Mexico from Europe two months earlier, launched the first of these northern revolts in the state of Nuevo León. Since most Mexicans still associated him with the Díaz regime, the general proved unable to attract a wide popular following. Consequently, by the end of December, Reyes's rebellion had fizzled out, and he was awaiting trial for treason in a Mexico City prison.

Soon after the government squelched the Reyes revolt, however, a former aide to Madero named Emilio Vásquez Gómez instigated a new uprising in Chihuahua. In late January 1912, Madero was dismayed to learn that Vásquez Gómez's forces had captured the major commercial and transportation center of Ciudad Juárez. Well aware that Chihuahuans held their famous native son, Pascual Orozco, in high esteem for his role in guiding the anti-Díaz forces to victory, Madero asked Orozco to take control of the government's campaign against Vásquez Gómez. Meeting with the rebel rank and file personally, Orozco was able to persuade his fellow Chihuahuans to lay down their arms in the name of national unity. But Madero's troubles were far from over. Just two months after quelling the Vásquez Gómez revolt, Orozco suddenly turned against the president in what would prove to be the most serious of the three northern uprisings against the beleaguered regime.

Relations between Orozco and Madero had been testy for some time. After Orozco's military triumph at Ciudad Juárez in May 1911, he had expected to be rewarded with a cabinet post or other high-level position in the Madero government. Instead, Madero had granted him the relatively minor post of commander of the Chihuahua rurales. While Orozco accepted the assignment, he never forgot that Madero denied him a more prestigious post. Why Orozco chose to break with Madero in March 1912, after helping him squelch the Vásquez Gómez revolt, is still debated among historians. Orozco claimed he split with the president because Madero had failed to fulfill the promises he made. Yet most scholars agree that Orozco's own political aspirations were probably the driving force behind the split. Ambitious and shrewd, Orozco "was determined to be on the winning side," Frank McLynn notes.[5] As one contemporary critic observed regarding the opportunistic Orozco: "He is for Pascual Orozco, first, last and always."[6]

To drum up support among the lower classes for his revolt, Orozco issued the Plan Orozquista, which promised higher wages for workers and the prompt return of illegally seized lands to villages. As he had hoped, discontented workers and small farmers throughout his home state were drawn to his populist platform. By the end of March, the Chihuahuan leader had amassed an army of several thousand that was headed toward Mexico City. With the rebels moving ever closer to the national capital, Madero placed the notoriously brutal yet skilled federal army general Victoriano Huerta in charge of a major new government offensive against Orozco. In late May, Huerta decisively defeated Orozco's outnumbered and out-gunned forces, thereby saving Madero's tottering regime—at least for the time being.

A RIGHT-WING PLOT

The defeat of Orozco's army did not bring an end to social unrest in Mexico. Throughout the remainder of 1912, labor

strikes were common. In the countryside, "frustrated peasants took land, looted homes, and murdered the wealthy
hacendados who had so oppressed them," Eileen Welsome
notes.[7] In the south, Zapata's scattered guerrilla bands had
proven all but impossible to eradicate. In the north, various
rebel groups carried out hit-and-run assaults on isolated federal units and outposts.

By year's end, Madero's failure to browbeat the unruly
peasantry into submission or ban the troublesome labor unions
altogether, as Díaz had done, led many upper-class Mexicans to
conclude that the president was too weak to protect their property and revive the nation's economy. At the same time, some
high-ranking army officials were coming to a similar conclusion.
An idealistic political reformer and intellectual like Madero
was not what their strife-torn country needed, they believed.
Instead, Mexico required a strongman president capable of
commanding the obedience of the lower classes and restoring law and order; in essence, a leader in the tradition of their
former commander-in-chief, Porfirio Díaz. In February 1913,
Mexican conservatives would get their strongman president
in the person of Victoriano Huerta, the same general Madero
had entrusted with quashing the Orozco rebellion.

The original instigators of the military coup that brought
Huerta to power in February were two old enemies of Madero:
General Bernardo Reyes, who had conspired to overthrow
the president in December 1911, and the deposed dictator's
nephew, General Félix Díaz, who led a short-lived rebellion
against Madero in the port city of Veracruz in October 1912.
Madero had placed both traitors in nearby federal peniten-
tiaries in Mexico City. By late January 1913, assisted by sym-
pathetic army officers who acted as go-betweens, Díaz and
Reyes had hatched a new joint plot against Madero. Díaz and
Reyes also invited Huerta, whose disdain for the president
was well known within military circles, to be part of their
conspiracy. Although Huerta declined their offer, he did not

inform Madero—or any of the president's military or civilian supporters—of the plot.

Shortly before dawn on February 9, 1913, Reyes and Díaz's collaborators in the army broke in and released the rebel leaders from prison. The generals, accompanied by nearly 2,000 renegade troops, marched straight to the National Palace in the heart of Mexico City. As the rebels closed in on the palace, the presidential guards opened fire with machine guns, killing several hundred attackers, including Bernardo Reyes. Díaz quickly retreated with his battered troops to the Ciudadela, an obsolete armory about 1.5 miles (2.5 km) away. When Madero discovered a short while later that the commander of Mexico City's loyalist forces had been wounded during the attack, he made what would turn out to be a fatal error: He accepted Huerta's offer to head the federal campaign to put down the mutiny.

THE DECENA TRÁGICA

For most of the next week and a half, later dubbed the *Decena Trágica* ("Ten Tragic Days"), a large federal force under Huerta exchanged artillery fire with Díaz's 1,500 troops in the Ciudadela. The lengthy cannon duel destroyed much of downtown Mexico City, and hundreds of innocent civilians were killed or wounded. Adding to the suffering of the city's beleaguered residents, food became scarce in the capital and the price of corn and other staples skyrocketed. Yet, day after day, the fighting ground on without resolution. "Loyalists should have won an easy victory," Michael Gonzales maintains. "Rebels—surrounded, outnumbered, and short on supplies— could not hold out for long. Victory over rebel troops was not, however, Huerta's objective."[8]

Early in the Decena Trágica, Huerta had secretly met with Felix Díaz to inform him that he had decided to join his rebellion. The two conspirators agreed to continue their devastating artillery exchange long enough to ensure that the people of Mexico City would become "desperate for a solution to the crisis," historians Meyer and Beezley contend.[9] On February 18, Huerta and Díaz, urged on by U.S. ambas-

AMERICA'S ROGUE DIPLOMAT IN MEXICO

Historians rank Henry Lane Wilson, the U.S. ambassador to Mexico from 1910 to 1913, among the worst high-level diplomats in U.S. history. A great admirer of Porfirio Díaz, Ambassador Wilson loathed Francisco Madero, because he was unwilling to use intimidation and violence to maintain order in Mexico as Díaz had done and because he supported raising taxes on foreign businesses, particularly the highly lucrative oil industry.

Wilson was under strict orders from President William Howard Taft to stay out of Mexico's internal affairs. As the Decena Trágica unfolded in mid-February 1913, however, the ambassador decided that he had found the perfect excuse to try to remove Madero from office. Arguing that Madero was incapable of restoring order to the beleaguered capital, Wilson urged the Spanish, British, and German foreign ministers to join him in formally calling for the president's resignation. Incensed by Wilson's highhanded behavior, Madero sent an indignant telegram to the U.S. State Department, accusing the American ambassador of "overstepping his proper diplomatic bounds," Frank McLynn writes.*

Although State Department officials reprimanded Wilson for meddling in Mexico's domestic politics, it did not stop the renegade ambassador from carrying on clandestine talks with Victoriano Huerta and Félix Díaz, either of whom he

sador to Mexico Henry Lane Wilson, who believed a right-wing military dictatorship would better protect U.S. business interests in Mexico than Madero's regime, were finally ready

believed would provide a better economic climate for U.S. business interests in Mexico than Madero. On the evening of February 18, just hours after Díaz and Huerta's henchmen arrested Madero at gunpoint, Wilson helped the two traitors hammer out a political agreement in a secret meeting at the U.S. Embassy in Mexico City. According to what came to be dubbed the *Pacto de la Embajada* ("Embassy Pact"), Huerta would act as provisional president until new national elections could be organized, at which time Díaz would be allowed to run unopposed for the presidency.

The following day, Madero's frantic wife, Sara, came to the U.S. Embassy to plead with Wilson to intervene with Huerta on her husband's behalf. Taking a very different tone from the one he had adopted over the last 10 days, Wilson informed Sara Madero that it would be inappropriate for him to interfere in the domestic concerns of a sovereign nation. After Madero was killed on the night of February 22, allegedly while trying to escape, the ambassador advised the State Department to accept Huerta's public explanation of the president's death, which Wilson personally considered to be "a closed incident."** After learning of Wilson's involvement in the coup, the new U.S. president, Woodrow Wilson, sent his personal envoy, John Lind, to Mexico and dismissed Ambassador Wilson on July 17, 1913.

---

* Frank McLynn, *Villa and Zapata: A History of the Mexican Revolution*. New York: Carroll & Graf Publishers, 2000, p. 155.
** Quoted in John S.D. Eisenhower, *Intervention! The United States and the Mexican Revolution, 1913–1917*. New York: W.W. Norton, 1993, p. 30.

Downed power lines and destroyed buildings are seen in Mexico City during the "Ten Tragic Days" of revolt against President Francisco Madero's government, which lasted from February 9 to February 19, 1913.

to make their move. Declaring that Madero was too incompetent to end the violence besetting the capital and agreeing that Huerta would act as Mexico's interim president until a new national election could be arranged, the rebels placed the shocked president under house arrest.

Three days later, while Madero and his former vice president, José María Pino Suárez, were being transported from the National Palace to a nearby federal penitentiary, both men were dragged from their cars and shot execution style by their military escorts. Huerta immediately announced that the two prisoners had been killed while trying "to escape."[10] With the tragic conclusion of Francisco Madero's troubled presidency on February 22, 1913, the Mexican Revolution began a new phase that was even more divisive and violent than its first 16 months had been.

5

Huerta and His Enemies

Long considered one of the great villains of Latin American history, General Victoriano Huerta governed Mexico with an iron fist as its interim president from February 1913 to July 1914. Derisively dubbed *El Chacal*—"the Jackal"—for his brutality and opportunism, Huerta was widely disdained within and outside his homeland as a political usurper and the likely mastermind behind Francisco Madero's murder. Hoping to reestablish a Díaz-style dictatorship backed by wealthy hacendados, big business, and the might of the federal army, Huerta quickly discovered that the tide of revolution could not be so easily reversed.

MEXICO'S CONTROVERSIAL NEW LEADER

José Victoriano Huerta Márquez was born in 1854 to Huichol Indian parents in Colotlán, in the west-central state of Jalisco.

Intelligent and driven, Victoriano learned to read and write at an early age. When he was just 16, an army general who happened to be passing through Colotlán recruited him to serve as his personal secretary. A few years later, the general helped his bright young protégé gain admittance to Mexico's most prestigious military academy. Rising rapidly through the ranks of the federal army, Huerta was made a general by Porfirio Díaz. One of the dictator's most trusted commanders, Huerta was known for his courage on the battlefield and his utter ruthlessness in dealing with opponents. As time went on, he also became notorious for his heavy drinking habits. Pancho Villa, who fought with Huerta to quell Pascual Orozco's rebellion in 1912, contemptuously nicknamed the general *el borrachito*—"the little drunkard." "Not once in all the times I spoke with him was he altogether sober," Villa wrote of Huerta in his memoirs, "for he drank morning, afternoon, and night."[1]

Despite the widespread public outcry over Huerta's illegal power grab and probable complicity in Madero's death, the general had some powerful backers in Mexico as of February 1913. Most important, the federal army's officer corps was thrilled to have a fellow soldier in the National Palace again. The majority of the landowning elite also backed Huerta in hopes that a strongman president would prove a more reliable protector of their property against rebellious peasants and workers than Madero had been.

Keeping the peace in the Mexican countryside, however, would be an even greater challenge for Huerta than it had been for his predecessor. In southern Mexico, the bloodshed and turmoil that had plagued the region toward the end of Díaz's rule and under Madero's short-lived presidency only worsened during Huerta's tenure. Convinced that Huerta would never force his wealthy hacendado supporters to return confiscated Indian properties, Emiliano Zapata and his followers intensified their attacks on federal outposts and railroads and executed the emissaries Huerta sent to Morelos to negotiate an end to the violence. During the first months of his presidency, Huerta deployed thousands of federal troops to Morelos and its neighboring states. Yet, despite Huerta's concerns about the Zapatistas to the south of Mexico City, it was becoming evident by the spring of 1913 that the fledgling regime confronted a much graver threat to its authority in the north.

The first indication that the Huerta administration was in serious trouble in northern Mexico came shortly after Madero's death in late February, when Governor Venustiano Carranza of Coahuila, a politically liberal hacendado, refused to recognize the new regime. The following month, the renegade governor issued a revolutionary call to arms, the Plan of Guadalupe, in honor of the hacienda where the document was composed. The Plan of Guadalupe boldly announced the creation of a national "Constitutionalist" army, with Carranza as its top commander or "First Chief." According to the self-styled "First Chief's" manifesto, once his Constitutionalist army had forced Huerta from office, Carranza would serve as Mexico's provisional president until fair and open national elections could be arranged.

Carranza's anti-Huerta campaign quickly gained recruits not only in Coahuila but also in Sonora, where Carranza established his new headquarters in July 1913 after suffering several military setbacks in his home state. Sonora was a logical place for Carranza to seek refuge—the state's government had supported the Constitutionalist cause from the first, even sending a representative to Coahuila to sign the plan before the document's official release on March 26.

At about the same time that Carranza fled Coahuila for Sonora, Álvaro Obregón, a middling farmer and talented amateur soldier who had helped put down Orozco's rebellion a year earlier, was appointed head of Constitutionalist military operations in that state. By the following summer, he had managed to drive the federal army out of most of Sonora. Obregón's troops included other middle-class Sonoran farmers and ranchers like himself, who feared Huerta would revive the stranglehold the

A circa-1923 photo of Álvaro Obregón. During the Mexican Revolution, he led troops that successfully drove the Mexican federal army out of the state of Sonora.

central government and a handful of wealthy hacendados and mine owners had exercised over their state under Díaz. The bulk of Obregón's force, however, consisted of poorer Sonorans, landless Indians, and disgruntled mine workers. Even though the Plan of Guadalupe, mirroring Carranza's own conservative social views, ignored the issues of land redistribution and workers' rights, the poorest sectors of society dominated the Constitutionalist ranks in Coahuila. Just as they had when they fought Díaz under Madero's banner, the impoverished farmers and laborers who formed the backbone of the movement in 1913 hoped a new regime would finally bring them their long-denied economic self-sufficiency and social justice.

THE RETURN OF PANCHO VILLA

By the time Carranza announced the founding of the Constitutionalist army at Guadalupe in late March, another revolutionary army devoted to toppling Huerta was emerging in the mineral-rich neighboring state of Chihuahua. Its organizer was one of the best-known and most colorful leaders of Madero's campaign to oust Díaz in 1911: Pancho Villa.

Villa's "simple creed demanded personal loyalty above nearly all else," historian John Eisenhower contends, and consequently he despised the treacherous Jackal for betraying his commander-in-chief.[2] Aside from avenging the murder of *Maderito* ("little Madero"), as Villa affectionately referred to the slain president, by declaring war on Huerta, Villa also saw a chance to settle an old score of his own with the general.[3] When his fellow Chihuahuan, Pascual Orozco, rebelled in the spring of 1912, Villa had volunteered to assist Huerta in stamping out the revolt, even though he thought of the federal army general as an incompetent drunkard. Toward the end of the campaign against Orozco, Huerta, incensed by Pancho's thinly veiled contempt for him, charged Villa with stealing an army horse, a crime punishable by death. At the last minute, Madero granted Villa a reprieve from the firing squad, but Huerta still insisted on throwing Villa into prison. After languishing in jail for six months, Villa escaped in December and fled across the U.S. border to El Paso. He would not return to his homeland until March 6, 1913, two weeks after Maderito's brutal murder.

When Villa slipped back across the Rio Grande into Mexico on the night of March 6 to overthrow the traitorous Huerta and avenge Madero's death, just eight armed supporters accompanied him. But as he rode south into the Chihuahuan countryside, Villa immediately began to attract large numbers of followers. By summer, he had enlisted several thousand cowboys, miners, oilfield workers, and small farmers to fight in his new revolutionary army. Villa was particularly success-ful at recruiting soldiers from the lowest rungs of Chihuahuan society. A legend that had been building around Villa ever since the rebellion against Porfirio Díaz helped draw the poor and oppressed to his army in 1913. According to the popular tradi-tion, during his prerevolutionary days as a bandit, Villa had been careful to only steal from the very wealthy. Never forgetting his own humble origins, he generously shared the money and goods he pilfered from his upper-class victims with Chihuahua's and Durango's most destitute families. Whether accurate or not, Villa's reputation as a latter-day Robin Hood who took from the rich to give to the poor had made him a hero among northern Mexico's impoverished masses.

The federal army maintained an especially large presence in Chihuahua because of the state's extensive mineral resources and strategic location between two early hotbeds of revolu-tionary activity, Coahuila and Sonora. Nevertheless, by the late summer, Villa felt confident that his new rebel army, soon to be dubbed the *División del Norte* ("Division of the North"), was ready to move beyond hit-and-run guerrilla attacks on isolated federal targets and engage the enemy directly on the battlefield. His optimism proved well founded. In a series of stunning victories beginning in August 1913, Villa and his men captured one key Chihuahuan city and transportation center after another, including Ciudad Juárez. By the end of the year, the División del Norte controlled the entire state, and Villa had been proclaimed Chihuahua's provisional governor. Many factors contributed to the rebels' success. Among them were Villa's innovative use of hijacked railcars to move his troops and horses quickly from one city to another and his troops' immense loyalty to him, a loyalty based on his considerable personal magnetism as well as his practice of paying his soldiers generously. To raise money for their wages, weapons, and ammunition, Villa had his troops hold up federal trains passing through Chihuahua, including one carrying a massive Wells Fargo silver shipment, and confiscate thousands of heads of cattle from local hacendados to sell across the border in Texas.

No fan of Carranza's, Villa refused to commit to more than a loose military alliance with the Constitutionalist army, despite Carranza's repeated efforts to bring Villa's troops under his direct command. When Carranza's emissaries first approached Villa in the late summer of 1913, the División del Norte was already the largest, best-equipped revolutionary force in Mexico, with a crack cavalry unit and a well-outfitted artillery division. Yet, although the División del Norte outstripped his army in firepower and manpower, Carranza still expected Villa to recognize him as head of the national anti-Huerta movement. At first Villa merely scoffed at Carranza's audacity, but after more consideration, he "realized that Carranza's Plan of Guadalupe offered Mexico a political platform that he himself totally lacked," John Eisenhower notes.[4] Moreover, in sharp contrast to Carranza, Villa, who believed his lack of a formal education made him unfit for the presidency, harbored no national political ambitions of his own. In the end, therefore, he decided to acknowledge Carranza as the rebellion's supreme political leader in the name of promoting revolutionary unity. At the same time, however, Villa made it clear that he would not tolerate interference from the "high and mighty" First Chief within his own military sphere of action.[5] "If I need generals," Villa curtly informed Carranza's emissaries, "I will appoint them myself."[6]

"THAT LOWDOWN BADMAN HUERTA"

Huerta's initial response to the growing military insurgency led by Villa, Obregón, and Carranza in the north and Zapata in the south was to vastly increase the size of the federal army. To meet the president's high new quotas for troops, officials in towns and villages across Mexico resorted to kidnapping able-bodied men wherever they could find them: in the fields, on their way to market, and at public gatherings of all sorts. In some cities, including the national capital, women were also snatched off the streets to toil in federal ammunition factories. The wife of an American diplomat stationed in Mexico City wrote in 1913:

> After the bullfight on Sunday, seven hundred unfortunates were seized, doubtless never to see their families again. . . . At a big fire a few days ago nearly a thousand were taken, many women among them, who are put to work in the [gun] powder mills. A friend told me this morning that the father, mother, two brothers, and the sister of one of her servants were taken last week. They scarcely dare, any of them, to go out after dark. Posting a letter may mean, literally going to the cannon's mouth.[7]

Huerta's ruthless conscription methods created immense bitterness among the Mexican people. In Morelos, where thousands of field hands and millworkers were forcibly shipped off to northern Mexico to help defeat Villa's growing rebel movement in Chihuahua, the injustice of *la leva* ("the draft") was the subject of "The Crimes of the Tyrant Huerta," a popular song:

The draft, the hateful draft,
That sowed desolation
On the whole beloved soil
Of our noble Nation.

The worker, the artisan,
The merchant and the peon,
They carried them off to the ranks,
Without any compassion.

He sent them to the North,
That lowdown badman Huerta,
To die unjustly
On the fields of battle. . . .[8]

AN ASSASSINATION AND A SHAM ELECTION

With popular resentment over his ruthless policies intensifying, Huerta became ever more dictatorial during the autumn of 1913, exiling critical journalists and building an extensive spy network to monitor the activities of his political opponents. Officeholders suspected of posing a threat to Huerta's autocratic rule were imprisoned. In some cases, individuals were kidnapped and murdered by the president's henchmen. The most notorious of these political assassinations occurred in September, after a respected senator from the state of Chiapas, Belisario Domínguez, daringly attacked Huerta in an open letter to his fellow congressmen. Blasting the president as "a bloody and ferocious soldier who assassinates without hesitation anyone who is an obstacle to his wishes," Domínguez called for Huerta's immediate ouster.[9] Domínguez closed his inflammatory message by urging his readers to distribute copies of the letter to newspaper editors, government officials, and ordinary citizens within their home districts. Shortly after the letter began to circulate in the capital, Huerta's secret agents abducted Domínguez from his Mexico City apartment and drove him to a nearby cemetery. There they shot the senator repeatedly and threw his body in a shallow grave.

Domínguez's sudden disappearance and the discovery of his bullet-ridden corpse a few days later horrified his fellow legislators. They overwhelmingly approved a resolution demanding that the president give a full account of the senator's death. In response, Huerta angrily dissolved Congress and ordered the arrests of nearly 100 legislators as enemies of the government. Two weeks later, on October 26, the Jackal ran unopposed in the first presidential elections to be held since the February coup against Madero.

During the Decena Trágica, Huerta had made a secret pact with his co-conspirator, Félix Díaz, regarding the presidential elections. If Díaz let him assume the reins of government immediately as interim chief executive, Huerta pledged that he would ensure that the national election went in Díaz's favor. Six months later, it became clear that Huerta intended to run in the October election despite his earlier promise. Fearful for his life, Díaz meekly bowed out of the contest and went on a self-imposed exile in the United States. In the purely-for-show autumn election, voter turnout fell well short of the legal requirements set by the Mexican Constitution, meaning that Huerta's inevitable victory at the polls was declared null and void. Unfazed, the general announced he would continue as Mexico's provisional president until new national elections were held the following summer.

PRESIDENT WILSON GETS INVOLVED

While the Jackal's tyrannical behavior was turning ever more Mexicans against him, it was also earning him the enmity of the new chief executive of the United States, President Woodrow Wilson (no relation to Ambassador Henry Lane Wilson). President Wilson, who was sworn into office just two weeks after Madero's murder, was outraged by the Mexican leader's assassination, which he blamed on Huerta. Although most other Western heads of state immediately recognized the general as Mexico's acting president, Wilson refused to accept the legitimacy of Huerta's rule. "I will not recognize a government of butchers," he fumed privately.[10]

Wilson, convinced that Lane Wilson had played an "evil part" in Madero's death, ignored the ambassador's repeated pleas to formally recognize the new regime that he had covertly helped to put in power during the Decena Trágica.[11] Highly skeptical of the ambassador's depiction of Huerta as a sincere supporter of democratic principles, Wilson decided in April 1913 to send his speechwriter and trusted friend, William Bayard Hale, to Mexico City to find out what was really going on in the National Palace and the U.S. Embassy. Working undercover, Hale concluded that Huerta was an autocrat and unstable alcoholic and that the general's staunch defender, Lane Wilson, was a shameless liar. The president immediately recalled Ambassador Wilson and sent a special emissary to Mexico City to present an ultimatum to Huerta: The U.S. government would continue to withhold formal recognition of Huerta's administration (meaning that obtaining weapons or loans from U.S. companies and banks would remain virtually impossible) until genuinely fair and open presidential elections were held.

After Huerta dissolved Congress and scared off all viable competitors in the presidential election of late October, President Wilson became more determined than ever to unseat the Jackal, even if it meant resorting to force. In his report to Wilson regarding Huerta, Hale had pointed out that it was, above all, the large revenues from Mexican oil exports that allowed the dictator to purchase the imported weapons he needed to defeat the rebels and remain in power. One strategy to unseat Huerta, therefore, would be to drive the federals out of Mexico's top seaports, thereby drastically reducing both the country's lucrative oil export trade and its ability to import foreign-made armaments.

THE INVASION OF VERACRUZ

In April 1914, with rebel forces pushing ever closer to Mexico City, Wilson decided it was time to drive the faltering federal army out of Veracruz, Mexico's leading seaport and the chief trading post for weapons coming in from Europe. Wilson's pretext for invading Veracruz was a minor incident that had occurred earlier that month in Tampico, another port on the Gulf of Mexico, where the U.S. Navy sustained a large presence to safeguard American investments in the region's vast oil fields. On April 9, possibly because rumors of approaching rebel forces had put them on edge, federal troops in Tampico detained eight American sailors who had come ashore to purchase supplies. On being informed of the arrests, the local federal commander immediately ordered the sailors' release. That, however, was not good enough for Admiral Henry Mayo, commander of the U.S. Atlantic Fleet off Tampico. Among other things, Mayo demanded that the Mexican commander severely punish the men responsible for the "hostile act" against the U.S. Navy and fire a 21-gun salute to the American flag.[12] When Huerta huffily rejected Mayo's demands, Wilson decided to use this alleged insult as an excuse to seize the port of Veracruz, where, it just so happened, a German ship laden with European armaments was expected to arrive on April 21.

On that day, Wilson ordered two divisions of the Atlantic Fleet to intercept the German ship before it could dock and also take control of the Veracruz customs house, to prevent future deliveries of imported weapons. The Americans had expected little resistance in Veracruz, but to their dismay 1,000 Mexican troops—mostly young cadets from the local Naval Academy—assisted by dozens of ordinary citizens, fought back against what they saw as an unprovoked attack on their city. By the evening of April 22, Veracruz had fallen to the Americans, but at a cost of 90 U.S. casualties and an estimated 300 Mexican casualties, including many innocent civilians. Mexicans all over the republic were outraged.

As a result of the Tampico Affair, the U.S. Navy invaded Mexico and occupied the Mexican port city of Veracruz in 1914 on the orders of President Woodrow Wilson. The U.S. occupation caused the breakdown of diplomatic relations between the two countries for a brief period.

Huerta, seeing an opportunity, attempted to use the public outcry against the U.S. invasion and subsequent six-month occupation of Veracruz to rally the Mexican people behind him. But the general's efforts came to nothing, since most rebel leaders condemned the American assault on Veracruz every bit as loudly as Huerta had. Despite their denunciations of Wilson's interference in Mexican affairs, however, the revolutionaries clearly benefited from the U.S. president's actions. Huerta and his government were not only denied lucrative custom-house revenues as long as U.S. forces occupied Veracruz, but the crisis also diverted the Mexican government's attention from the ongoing battle against the Zapatistas in the south and the Constitutionalists in the north. By the early summer of 1914, with the revolutionary forces moving ever closer to the capital city, it was becoming increasingly apparent that the Jackal's days in power were numbered.

Revolutionary Civil War

By June 1914, virtually all of Mexico had fallen under rebel control following a string of Constitutionalist victories, most notably by Pancho Villa to the north of Mexico City and Álvaro Obregón on the west coast. On July 15, 1914, realizing his military position was hopeless, Victoriano Huerta resigned as provisional president and fled the country for Spain. Soon after his departure, Constitutionalist troops led by General Obregón occupied Mexico City.

With Huerta out of the way, long-standing rivalries and ideological differences among the various revolutionary leaders came to the fore. Neither Villa nor Emiliano Zapata had ever had much patience with Venustiano Carranza, the self-styled "First Chief" of the Constitutionalist army, whom they considered arrogant and self-serving. Indeed, Zapata—convinced that the wealthy hacendado would not implement any meaningful land redistribution—had refused to recognize Carranza as the head of the anti-Huerta campaign, despite repeated overtures from the Constitutionalists. At one point, he even suggested that Carranza be shot for naming himself as First Chief of the revolutionary movement since he had no genuine respect for its core principles.

To Zapata's disgust, Carranza made himself Mexico's new provisional president following Huerta's ouster. Carranza, Zapata then proclaimed, must start carrying out the radical reforms outlined in the Plan of Ayala at once if the First Chief expected to win his endorsement as interim president. When Carranza refused, explaining that the plan violated hacendado property rights, Zapata angrily denounced him. Villa, who had become increasingly resentful of Carranza's condescending attitude toward him in recent months, quickly followed suit, blasting Carranza for his indifference to the needs of the common people.

At this juncture, a worried Obregón decided to assume the role of peacemaker. Although he disliked Villa and considered Zapata's ideas too radical, the general was eager to avoid an immediate outbreak of hostilities between the battle-weary Constitutionalist army and the combined forces of the two rebel leaders. Obregón suggested that representatives of the various revolutionary factions meet to resolve their differences and form a coalition government. Villa immediately embraced Obregón's proposal. Zapata required a bit more convincing but eventually agreed to send delegates to the "Revolutionary Convention," scheduled to open in the city of Aguascalientes on October 10, 1914.

Carranza only agreed to Obregón's proposal to open formal talks with the upstart Zapatistas and Villistas (as Villa's followers had become known) with the greatest reluctance. Because he made little effort to encourage his supporters to attend the Aguascalientes conference, Villistas and Zapatistas, along with the most radical, independent-minded wing of the Constitutionalist party, held a sizable majority at the Revolutionary Convention. Their contempt for the authority of Carranza became apparent when the delegates passed a resolution declaring the convention to be a completely sovereign, or self-governing body.[1] After endorsing the Plan of Ayala as the basis for the nation's agrarian policy, the delegates resolved that the best way to heal the fissures within the revolutionary movement was for Carranza to renounce the presidency at once. Proclaiming the convention as Mexico's legitimate government, they appointed a minor revolutionary general, Eulalio Gutiérrez, as interim president. Gutiérrez, in turn, appointed Villa, as the head of the single largest rebel force, commander-in-chief of the newly created Army of the Convention.

Carranza, however, was not about to give up so easily. Repudiating the convention's authority, he announced that he intended to remain Mexico's chief executive until new national elections could be organized. In late November, Carranza and his Constitutionalist backers, including his ablest commander, Obregón, abandoned Mexico City. While Obregón concentrated on rebuilding the Constitutionalist army, Carranza established a government-in-exile in Veracruz. The bustling gulf port proved a wise choice for his provisional capital. For one thing, the U.S. occupying force, which had only recently vacated the city, had left behind an enormous stockpile of weapons and ammunition seized from Huerta's army. For another, control of the port meant that the Constitutionalists could use the hefty revenues from the Veracruz customs house and the area's nearby oil fields to bankroll their military campaigns against the Conventionalists.

Shortly after Carranza and Obregón departed Mexico City, the Zapatistas and Villistas moved into the capital. On December 6, the two groups' famous leaders held a huge joint parade through the capital's streets to the National Palace. To Provisional President Gutiérrez's immense irritation, Villa and

In one of the most famous images of the Mexican Revolution, revolution-ary leaders Pancho Villa *(center)* and Emiliano Zapata *(next to Villa, right, with sombrero on knee)* are photographed at the Presidential Palace in Mexico City in 1914.

Zapata not only neglected to consult with him personally, but they also commandeered the presidential office for a photo session from which he was excluded. A few weeks after this humiliating episode, Gutiérrez decided to abandon Mexico City for San Luis Potosí, where he finally resigned the following summer without ever having exerted any real influence over the Conventionalist movement or its independent-minded military leaders.

CONVENTIONALISTS
VERSUS CONSTITUTIONALISTS

When they finally met for the first time in early December 1914, Villa and Zapata immediately found common ground in their disdain for the Constitutionalists' leadership. The Constitutionalist leaders were pampered "men who have always slept on soft pillows," Villa accused, and had no genuine sympathy for the plight of the masses. Zapata went even further, blasting Carranza and Obregón as "the scourge of the people. . . . As soon as they see a little chance, well, they want to take advantage of it and line their own pockets!"[2]

Zapata and Villa were in complete agreement regarding the failings of the Constitutionalists' top officials. Nonetheless, to the detriment of the Conventionalist cause, the two generals' alliance proved fleeting. The coalition had already begun to unravel by mid-December, when Zapata heard reports that some of Villa's most influential backers had suggested it might be "necessary to eliminate him" on account of his radical land reform program.[3] Villa's actions only lent credence to the disturbing rumors. Villa dragged his feet in sending Zapata promised artillery, and even worse, ordered the execution of Zapata's longtime political adviser and chief delegate to the Aguascalientes Convention, journalist Paulino Martínez, supposedly as punishment for Martínez's past criticism of Madero. By the end of December, a disillusioned Zapata, accompanied by most of his peasant army, had returned to Morelos, where he carried out his revolutionary land redistribution program and defended his home state from Constitutionalist incursions.

While Villa consolidated his military position in northern Mexico during the winter of 1915, Carranza and Obregón expanded their side's popularity. Michael Gonzales writes: "Carranza and Obregón, displaying superior political and organizational skills, developed a clear political strategy centered around nationalism and social reformism calculated to win the support of workers, peasants, and the middle class."[4]

Eager to co-opt the Villistas' popular appeal, Carranza and Obregón proclaimed their support for labor and land reforms, new restrictions on foreign-owned businesses, and a more equitable tax system. After tens of thousands of new recruits, drawn by these promises of social and economic reform, joined Carranza's army, Villa publicly denounced the Constitutionalist leader as a phony and a hypocrite. Villa's accusations, however, had little impact on Carranza's growing appeal among the Mexican masses. By early 1915, Carranza, with great fanfare, had begun to grant small tracts of public land to needy peasants near his headquarters in Veracruz. Villa, on the other hand, had yet to implement any kind of organized land redistribution program in his home base of Chihuahua.

OBREGÓN GETS THE BETTER OF VILLA

As spring approached, Obregón felt confident that his army, its ranks swollen by new peasant recruits, was ready to launch a major offensive against Villa's legendary División del Norte. Grossly underestimating Obregón, or *El Perfumado* ("the sissy"), as Villa liked to call him, Villa boldly moved his army into central Mexico to meet the Constitutionalists when they began to march north in late March. The two armies converged near the town of Celaya, about 100 miles (161 km) northwest of Mexico City. During the First and Second Battles of Celaya, (April 6 to 7 and April 13 to 15), Obregón drew on lessons gleaned from newspaper accounts of the First World War, which had erupted in Europe nearly a year earlier. When British and French cavalry and infantry units attempted frontal assaults on well-entrenched German troops armed with machine guns and long-range rifles, Obregón noted, they inevitably suffered terrible casualties. Since Villa was known to rely on massive frontal cavalry charges, Obregón deployed his heavily armed infantry at Celaya in trenches encircled by barbed-wire entanglements, from which they would be protected while mowing down Villa's advancing horsemen. Obregón's strategy worked only too well. By the end of the Second Battle of Celaya, an estimated 9,000 Villistas had been killed or wounded in the fighting. Just 400 casualties were reported by the victorious Constitutionalists.

On April 29, the two armies clashed again near León, about 50 miles (80 km) north of Celaya. Villa, having apparently learned nothing from his costly mistakes at Celaya, launched repeated frontal attacks against Obregón's entrenched troops, only to have his much-vaunted cavalry unit cut to pieces by Constitutionalist machine-gun and rifle fire. During the ferocious battle, which continued for more than five weeks before Villa's decimated force finally retreated northward on June 5, an artillery shell severed Obregón's right arm, and a reported 12,000 soldiers, the vast majority of them Villistas, were killed. A few weeks later, Obregón commanded the Constitutionalist forces against the División del Norte at Aguascalientes in what would prove to be Villa's last stand in central Mexico. Almost unbelievably, Villa once again sacrificed wave after wave of his cavalrymen in futile frontal attacks on Obregón's strategically placed barbed-wire entrenchments.

After the debacle at Aguascalientes, Villa and the remnants of his División del Norte retreated to their original stronghold of Chihuahua. His resources all but exhausted, Villa was reduced to raising funds for supplies and his soldiers' wages by raiding local haciendas and towns. On November 22, in a last-ditch effort to expand his military base into neighboring Sonora, Villa attacked the state capital of Hermosillo. Shortly after suffering yet another demoralizing rout at the hands of the enemy, this time at a cost of 2,000 dead, most of the División del Norte decided to accept Carranza's offer of a general amnesty and surrender. In the meantime, their former commander, accompanied by several hundred hard-core followers, vanished into the rugged foothills of western Chihuahua. Grimly determined to keep his anti-Carranza crusade alive against all odds, Villa waged a vicious guerrilla campaign from his remote mountain base against nearby Constitutionalist targets.

WILSON'S "UNTHINKABLE BETRAYAL"

It was not only the Constitutionalists whom Villa and his commandos harassed during the winter of 1915–1916. Villa also turned his wrath on U.S. companies and citizens in northern Mexico. At the root of Villa's anti-American rage was President Woodrow Wilson's official recognition of the Carranza regime on October 19, 1915, as Mexico's legitimate government and his concurrent embargo on U.S. arms shipments to Carranza's opponents. Anxious to avoid provoking his country's powerful neighbor, Villa had gone out of his way to protect U.S. property in Mexico during his military campaigns against Huerta and the Constitutionalists. In contrast to Carranza, he had even refrained from criticizing the U.S. takeover of Veracruz in April 1914. Consequently, Villa viewed Wilson's decision to throw the weight of his government behind Carranza and the Constitutionalists as "an unthinkable betrayal," Eileen Welsome contends.[5]

At the heart of Wilson's choice of Carranza over himself, Villa believed, was a treacherous secret pact the president had made with the First Chief. Villa was convinced that Carranza had offered Washington sweeping economic privileges in Mexico in exchange for financial and military assistance. In light of Carranza's ardent nationalism and Wilson's well-known commitment to the principle of open diplomacy, Villa's suspicions regarding a covert deal between the Constitutionalist leader and Wilson "seemed highly implausible," Michael Gonzales writes. "But . . . [Villa's] rabid anti-Americanism and hatred of Carranza led him to irrational conclusions."[6]

In truth, Wilson's decision to recognize Carranza was rooted more in political and military concerns than in economic ones, as Villa believed. By mid-1915, World War I had been raging for a year, and there was growing speculation in Europe that the United States would soon enter the conflict on the side of the Allies, composed chiefly of Great Britain, France, and Russia. This move was something that the

German high command wanted to avoid at all costs. Hoping to divert Washington's attention from the fighting in Europe, the Germans attempted to incite an international crisis in which the United States would be pitted against its politically unstable neighbor to the south. To that end, German agents secretly contacted Victoriano Huerta in Spain. They offered the exiled dictator money and armaments to renew his fight against the revolutionaries if he would agree to attack American property and civilians in Mexico. Huerta accepted and headed for southern Texas, where he planned to join forces with another embittered Mexican exile, Pascual Orozco, before sneaking across the border into his homeland. Texan authorities got wind of the conspiracy, however, and threw both men in prison, where the hard-drinking Huerta soon died of liver disease.

In the wake of the foiled conspiracy, Wilson worried that the Germans would inevitably try again to exploit Mexico's unsettled political situation for their own gain. Consequently, Wilson concluded that his administration had to help restore political stability in Mexico quickly. With the Constitutionalists gaining the upper hand on the battlefield, Wilson decided to back Carranza, despite Villa's friendlier stance toward the United States.

VILLISTAS ON THE RAMPAGE

To avenge what he viewed as Wilson's ingratitude toward him while at the same time creating diplomatic headaches for his hated rival, Carranza, Villa ordered his commandos to vandalize and loot American property and bully American citizens in Chihuahua and neighboring Sonora. On January 10, 1916, Villa took his hostility toward Washington to another level when his commandos pulled 16 Texan mining engineers off a train near Santa Isabel, Chihuahua, shot them in cold blood, and then stripped and mutilated their corpses. The brutal murders so inflamed public opinion in the United States that

El Paso was briefly put under martial law to keep irate Texans from seeking vengeance on innocent Mexican civilians across the Rio Grande in Ciudad Juárez.

Almost exactly two months after the Santa Isabel massacre, Villa decided to take his violent anti-Wilson crusade to the United States itself. Early on the morning of March 9, he sent 500 commandos across the Chihuahuan border into New Mexico to attack the U.S. Army garrison at Camp Furlong and terrorize the nearby town of Columbus. Although completely surprised by the predawn attack, the garrison's better-armed defenders soon drove off Villa's men under a hail of machine-gun and rifle fire.

Meanwhile, a large Villista raiding party was shooting, burning, and looting its way through the streets of Columbus. Shouting "¡Viva Villa!" and, according to some contemporary accounts, "¡Muerte a los gringos!" ("Death to the gringos!"), the raiders managed to torch most of the town and kill 10 people before U.S. troops from Camp Furlong finally galloped into Columbus shortly after daybreak.[7] Seriously outgunned, the Villistas retreated back across the border with the American cavalry in hot pursuit. In all, 18 Americans—8 of them soldiers— and more than 100 Villistas died as a result of the March 9 attack.

THE PUNITIVE EXPEDITION

As the first invasion of American territory since the War of 1812, the "raid on Columbus caused a sensation in the United States," Frank McLynn writes. Although "Wilson himself was reluctant to intervene in Mexico, as he thought this was to play both Villa's and Germany's game," the president "was up for election in the autumn and an angry Congress and enraged public opinion forced him to act."[8] Determined to avoid a full-scale war with Mexico, Wilson made a point of personally contacting Carranza to assure him that any military force he sent across the border would have just one goal: the capture of Pancho Villa.

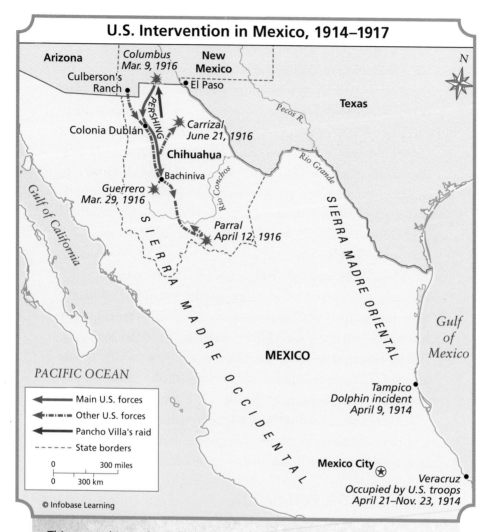

U.S. Intervention in Mexico, 1914–1917

Arizona

Columbus
Mar. 9, 1916

New
Mexico

N

Culberson's
Ranch

El Paso

Pecos R.

Texas

PERSHING

Carrizal
June 21, 1916

Colonia Dublán

Chihuahua

Rio Grande

Bachiniva

Rio Conchos

Guerrero
Mar. 29, 1916

SIERRA MADRE ORIENTAL

Parral
April 12, 1916

Gulf of California

SIERRA MADRE OCCIDENTAL

Gulf
of
Mexico

PACIFIC OCEAN

MEXICO

Tampico
Dolphin incident
April 9, 1914

← Main U.S. forces
←·—·—· Other U.S. forces
← Pancho Villa's raid
- - - - State borders

0   300 miles
0   300 km

Mexico City

Veracruz
Occupied by U.S. troops
April 21–Nov. 23, 1914

© Infobase Learning

This map shows the U.S. advances and campaigns undertaken during the Mexican Revolution. These U.S. actions were directed against Pancho Villa and his revolutionary supporters who, angered by American support for the oppressive Mexican government, had attacked the village of Columbus in New Mexico.

On March 15, 1916, one week after the Columbus raid, Wilson ordered the formation of a 5,000-man Punitive Expedition headed by the respected Army general John J.

Pershing to hunt down Villa in his home state of Chihuahua. An ill-conceived project from the start, the expedition was an unqualified failure for the U.S. Army and government. In sharp contrast to their American pursuers, Villa and his men "were veterans of guerrilla warfare and knew the terrain intimately," Michael Gonzales notes.[9] For nearly 11 months, a total of 12,000 U.S. troops wandered through hundreds of miles of rugged mountains and sun-baked deserts in Chihuahua without so much as catching a glimpse of their elusive prey.

Viewed by many Mexicans as an affront to their national pride, the Punitive Expedition provided a boost to Villa's dwindling popularity in his home state and throughout northern Mexico. By the end of 1916, pro-Villa and anti-American rioting had erupted in the southern Chihuahua city of Parral. To the dismay of Venustiano Carranza, the Villistas, their numbers swollen by new recruits, now occupied the state capital. In January 1917, to Carranza's great relief, Wilson finally decided it was time to cut American losses and bring the expeditionary force home. After devoting nearly $150 million to its fruitless campaign to nab Villa, however, Washington was loath to admit that the expedition had been a total bust. As Pershing began to march toward the border, government officials announced to a skeptical American public that New Mexicans and Texans could rest easier now. Though Villa remained at large, they declared, the crime-ridden border region from which he had launched his infamous raid had been successfully "cleaned up."[10]

Despite the popular sympathy for Villa that the Punitive Expedition aroused in Mexico, the military and political gains made by Villistas in Chihuahua during the failed U.S. campaign would prove fleeting. By early 1917, Carranza's authority was acknowledged virtually everywhere in war-weary Mexico, even in much of the belligerent Zapata's home state of Morelos,

(continues on page 86)

AIRPLANES AND THE
HUNT FOR PANCHO VILLA

At the start of the Punitive Expedition in March 1916, General John Pershing had held out great hopes for the mission's small airplane squadron. Those hopes, as it turned out, were completely unrealistic. Although the inventors of the airplane, Orville and Wilbur Wright, were Americans, airplane technology had been largely neglected in the United States in the years since the brothers made their first successful flight at Kitty Hawk, North Carolina, in 1903. In contrast, Europe had made significant strides in airplane technology, particularly since the outbreak of the First World War in 1914. The eight-plane First Aero Squadron assigned to Pershing's expedition in 1916 consisted entirely of flimsily constructed and notoriously underpowered JN-3 biplanes ("Jennies"). In war-torn Europe, on the other hand, German and British commanders had at their disposal considerably sturdier aircraft capable of climbing to altitudes of 15,000 feet (4,600 meters) and reaching speeds of more than 110 miles per hour (177 km per hour). While not a single plane in the First Aero Squadron was outfitted for combat, contemporary European military aircraft, equipped with machine guns that "fired through their propellers, . . . could engage in dogfights with each other and even perform bombardment missions," John Eisenhower writes.*

Although the First Aero Squadron was not expected to fly combat missions for the Punitive Expedition, Pershing hoped to use it in reconnaissance and liaison missions. Yet, to the enormous frustration of the squadron's commander, Captain Benjamin Foulois, the unreliable Jennies proved woefully inadequate even for these limited tasks in northern Mexico's rugged terrain. "The planes are not capable of

Lieutenant Carleton G. Chapman of the U.S. Signal Corps pre-
pares for takeoff at Casas Grandes, Chihuahua, Mexico, during
the Punitive Expedition into Mexico to capture Pancho Villa,
circa 1916.

meeting the present military needs, incident to this expedition," he complained shortly after arriving in Chihuahua:
"Their low power motors and limited climbing ability . . .
are no good around the mountains which cover the present theatre of operations."** By the end of the first week
of the mission, the squadron had lost two planes—one after
its pilot was forced to make a crash landing and the other
to engine failure. A month later, the squadron had been
reduced to just two fully operational planes. On April 20,
1916, the surviving Jennies were disassembled and returned
by truck to New Mexico. By this time Foulois and the fleet's
other pilots had flown more than 500 missions for General
Pershing. Only a relatively small number of the flights, however, had involved distances of more than 50 miles (80 km)
from their landing fields.

(continues)

(continued)

When the United States entered World War I on the Allied side in April 1917, just three months after Wilson withdrew Pershing's entire expeditionary force from Mexico, Washington dramatically increased government funding for the nation's fledgling air force. By the war's end in November 1918, the United States had sent 740 state-of-the-art combat aircraft to Western Europe to help defeat the Germans. In all, U.S. airplanes flew 150 bombing missions during World War I, downing more than 750 German aircraft in the process.

---

* John S.D. Eisenhower, *Intervention! The United States and the Mexican Revolution, 1913-1917*. New York: W.W. Norton, 1993, p. 254.

** Ibid., p. 256.

(continued from page 83)
which Constitutionalist troops had invaded the previous May. Nonetheless, although its bloodiest phase had come to an end, the Mexican Revolution was not quite over yet.

A Revolutionary
New Constitution

With most of Mexico under Constitutionalist control, Venustiano Carranza was optimistic in late 1916 that the violence and uncertainty of the past five years was finally over. In an effort to provide an institutional foundation for the political and social upheaval that had brought him to power, the provisional president decided to call a special convention in the city of Querétaro to review and revise the Mexican Constitution.

Anxious to keep radical social reforms out of the amended constitution, Carranza barred Zapatistas and Villistas from serving as convention delegates. Yet, to Carranza's dismay, even without the Zapatistas' and Villistas' influence, it soon became apparent that most delegates wanted a charter that did more than merely outline the fundamental political rights and duties of Mexican citizens and the federal government's different branches. They sought a constitution capable of addressing the glaring social and economic inequalities that had driven the Mexican masses to rebel in the first place.

The four most significant clauses of the constitution drafted by the Querétaro delegates in late 1916 and early 1917 are Article 3 on education; Article 27 on property rights and land reform; Article 123 on the rights of labor; and Article 130 on church-state relations. Insisting that all Mexicans, regardless of social class, had the inalienable right to a "democratic" education "maintained entirely apart from any religious doctrine," Article 3 stipulated for the first time in Mexican history that primary education should be free, mandatory, and secular. Clearly influenced by Zapata's Plan of Ayala, Article 27 authorized the state to confiscate and subdivide "large landed estates" and called for

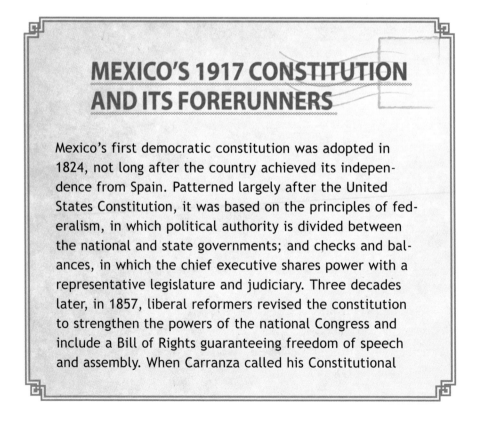

MEXICO'S 1917 CONSTITUTION AND ITS FORERUNNERS

Mexico's first democratic constitution was adopted in 1824, not long after the country achieved its independence from Spain. Patterned largely after the United States Constitution, it was based on the principles of federalism, in which political authority is divided between the national and state governments; and checks and balances, in which the chief executive shares power with a representative legislature and judiciary. Three decades later, in 1857, liberal reformers revised the constitution to strengthen the powers of the national Congress and include a Bill of Rights guaranteeing freedom of speech and assembly. When Carranza called his Constitutional

the return of communal lands illegally seized from Indian villages under Porfirio Díaz. The precedent-breaking article also put strict restrictions on land ownership by noncitizens and religious organizations such as the Roman Catholic Church, traditionally one of the nation's largest landholders. Article 27 also proclaimed national ownership of Mexico's subsoil resources, including its extensive silver, copper, and oil reserves. Directed at the country's long-exploited working class, Article 123 mandated that laborers be awarded a fair wage, one day off per week, an eight-hour workday, and the right to form unions and strike. It also established the principle of "equal wages" for "equal work, regardless of sex or nationality."[1]

The last of the four most famous provisions of the new constitution, Article 130, reflected the document's strong anticlerical tone. Rooted in the delegates' concern that conservative

Convention in 1916 following five years of nearly continuous civil war in Mexico, the Constitution of 1857—at least, technically—was still in effect.

The provisions in the 1917 Constitution regarding workers' and peasants' rights, national ownership of Mexico's natural resources, and strict separation of church and state represented a sharp break with the republic's two previous constitutions.

The new constitution also broke with earlier charters by strengthening the executive branch of the federal government at the expense of the legislative and judicial branches. According to the constitution's provisions, only the president may sign a bill into law. Additionally, the Constitution of 1917 gave the chief executive sweeping authority to issue *reglamentos*, or executive decrees, which had all the same legal power as laws.

Roman Catholic Church leaders would try to stifle meaningful social reform in Mexico, the anticlericalism of the constitution's authors was evident in many of the charter's clauses, including Article 27, with its stringent restrictions on land ownership by religious groups. Most significant, Article 130 banned clergymen from holding political office, forming political parties, or even voting, and declared that only the federal government could authorize the opening of new places of worship.

On February 5, 1917, Carranza proclaimed the formal adoption of Mexico's groundbreaking new constitution, which he had reluctantly signed a few days earlier. Although he privately considered many of the constitution's provisions, particularly those concerning rural land reform and the rights of labor, too radical, Carranza did find some aspects of the new charter appealing. The authoritarian leader was particularly pleased with the document's provisions regarding the executive branch, whose powers were significantly expanded. A fervent economic nationalist who resented the dominance of many key Mexican industries by foreign corporations and investors, Carranza also approved of the new constitution's restrictions on foreign land ownership and its insistence that Mexico's subsoil resources were the exclusive property of the Mexican state.

PRESIDENT CARRANZA

Carranza ran virtually unopposed in the special presidential election held one month after the new constitution was proclaimed. Carranza won handily at the polls, as the Mexican people closely associated him with the progressive document even though he actually had little influence on the charter's final form. After formally taking office on May 1, however, the former hacendado made it clear that he had no intention of implementing the constitution's radical social ideals. Dedicated nationalist that he was, the president was only too happy to comply with the stringent new limitations the constitution placed on land ownership by foreigners. Yet Carranza distributed just 500,000 acres (202,000 hectares) of land to the peasantry under the charter's groundbreaking Article 27. Five hundred thousand acres was "a paltry sum when one considers that many hacendados had more than this," note Michael Meyer, William Sherman, and Susan Deeds, and leading Chihuahuan hacendado Luis Terrazas "alone owned in excess of seven million acres [2.8 million ha]. In addition, the land Carranza did distribute had been taken away from his political enemies." Carranza's land policies, the authors maintain, represented "neither the spirit nor the intent of Article 27."[2]

The record of the Carranza administration on labor issues was no better than its record on agrarian reform. In 1918, in accordance with Article 123 of the constitution, the president grudgingly permitted the creation of Mexico's first nationwide union, the Confederación Regional de Obreros Mexicanos (Regional Confederation of Mexican Workers), or CROM. CROM proved unable to win any significant concessions for Mexico's heavily exploited workers during Carranza's presidency, however, despite the strongly pro-labor tenor of the constitution.

The restoration of Mexico's lucrative mineral exports under Carranza's presidency helped to diminish the terrible economic hardships of the chaotic civil war years, when silver, copper, and oil production plummeted by as much as 70 percent from prerevolutionary levels and agricultural shortages sent food prices soaring. Still, as Carranza continued to put off adoption of the sweeping social and economic reforms contained in the constitution, underpaid factory workers and miners and landless peasants across Mexico became ever more disgruntled with their new leader. And no Mexicans were more disgusted by Carranza's foot-dragging than Emiliano Zapata and his followers in Morelos.

(continues on page 94)

EXCERPTS FROM ARTICLE 27 OF THE MEXICAN CONSTITUTION

Hailed as one of the most progressive constitutions in modern political history, the Mexican Constitution of 1917 remains in use today, although it has been amended many times. Below are excerpts from what is often considered as the document's most radical clause, Article 27:

Article 27. . . . The Nation shall at all times have the right to impose on private property such limitations as the public interest may demand, as well as the right to regulate the utilization of natural resources which are susceptible of appropriation, in order to conserve them and to ensure a more equitable distribution of public wealth. With this end in view, necessary measures shall be taken to divide up large landed estates; to develop small landed holdings in operation; to create new agricultural centers, with necessary lands and waters; to encourage agriculture in general and to prevent the destruction of natural resources, and to protect property from damage to the detriment of society. Centers of population which at present either have no lands or water or which do not possess them in sufficient quantities for the needs of their inhabitants, shall be entitled to grants thereof, which shall be taken from adjacent properties, the rights of small landed holdings in operation being respected at all times.

 In the Nation is vested the direct ownership of all natural resources of the continental shelf and the submarine shelf of the islands; of all minerals or substances, which in veins, ledges, masses or ore pockets, form deposits of a nature distinct from the components of the earth itself, such as the minerals from which industrial metals and metalloids are extracted; deposits of precious stones . . . ; petroleum and all solid, liquid, and gaseous hydrocarbons. . . .

1. Only Mexicans by birth or naturalization and Mexican companies have the right to acquire ownership of lands, waters, and their appurtenances, or to obtain concessions for the exploitation of mines or of waters. The State may grant the same right to foreigners, provided they agree before the Ministry of Foreign Relations to consider themselves as nationals in respect to such property, and bind themselves not to invoke the protection of their governments in matters relating thereto; under penalty, in case of noncompliance with this agreement, of forfeiture of the property acquired to the Nation. Under no circumstances may foreigners acquire direct ownership of lands or waters within a zone of one hundred kilometers [62 miles] along the frontiers and of fifty kilometers [32 miles] along the shores of the country. . . .

2. Religious institutions known as churches, regardless of creed, may in no case acquire, hold, or administer real property or hold mortgages thereon; such property held at present either directly or through an intermediary shall revert to the Nation. . . . Places of public worship are the property of the Nation, as represented by the Federal Government, which shall determine which of them may continue to be devoted to their present purposes. . . .*

---

* "1917 Constitution of Mexico," http://www.ilst.edu/class/ hist263/docs/1917const.html#TitleI.

(continued from page 91)

THE DEATH OF ZAPATA

Throughout 1917 and 1918, Zapata and his loyal commandos continued to carry out guerrilla-style attacks on federal targets in Morelos. Concerned about the proximity of Zapata's home state to the national capital as well as the enduring appeal of his slogan of "land and liberty," Carranza felt he could not afford to ignore the ongoing challenge to his authority in Morelos. Yet, although he dispatched thousands of federal troops to Morelos to defeat the Zapatistas and terrorize their supporters (in some cases by burning down entire towns whose inhabitants were suspected of aiding the revolutionaries), Zapata managed to elude capture.

In March 1919, Carranza decided that he had had quite enough of the wily guerrilla chieftain after Zapata published an inflammatory and insulting open letter to him. Refusing to recognize the legitimacy of Carranza's claim to the presidency, Zapata scornfully addressed his letter to "Citizen Carranza":

> As the citizen I am, as a man with a right to think and speak aloud, as a peasant fully aware of the needs of the humble people, as a revolutionary and a leader of great numbers, . . . I address myself to you Citizen Carranza. . . . From the time your mind first generated the idea of revolution . . . and you conceived the idea of naming yourself Chief . . . you turned the struggle to your own advantage and that of your friends who helped you rise. . . . It never occurred to you that the Revolution was fought for the benefit of the great masses, for the legions of the oppressed whom you motivated by your great harangues. It was a magnificent pretext and a brilliant recourse for you to oppress and deceive. . . . In the agrarian matter you have given or rented our haciendas to your favor-ites. The old landholdings . . . have been taken over by new landlords . . . and the people mocked in their hopes.[3]

Until the end of his life, Emiliano Zapata continued to defend the rights of Mexican peasants through guerrilla attacks on federal targets. In 1919, the Carranza government ended the threat posed by Zapata by assassinating the revolutionary leader.

Determined to dispose of the troublesome Zapata once and for all, Carranza ordered his top general in Morelos, Pablo González, to assassinate the popular rebel leader. González, in turn, recruited the services of a charismatic but ruthless young colonel named Jesús María Guajardo. Guajardo wrote to Zapata, claiming that he and several hundred of his men wanted to desert the Federal Army and join forces with his guerrilla band. Although at first suspicious of the young federal officer, Zapata eventually agreed to meet Guajardo at the Hacienda de Chinameca in central Morelos on April 10, 1919.

Zapata, who took only a small contingent of 10 men with him to Chinameca, seems to have given little thought to the "honor guard" Guajardo had posted just inside the hacienda gate to meet him. As Zapata passed between their ranks, the guards suddenly raised their rifles simultaneously and opened fire. Zapata's bullet-ridden corpse was strapped onto a horse and taken to the Chinameca municipal hall, where it was placed on display as a grisly warning to his supporters. Soon after the assassination, a grateful Carranza promoted Guajardo to the rank of brigadier general. Deprived of its beloved leader, the beleaguered Zapatista movement died out in Morelos, just as Carranza had hoped. What he had not foreseen, however, was the intense backlash that his treacherous act would elicit among the Mexican public.

OBREGÓN CHALLENGES CARRANZA

Because most Mexicans assumed that the president was behind the assassination of his hated rival, Zapata's murder at Chinameca, while "elevating" the slain 39-year-old reformer "to martyrdom," at the same time "greatly lowered Carranza in the public esteem," historians Michael Meyer and William Beezley observe.[4] With the national elections of 1920 approaching, Álvaro Obregón, who had long coveted the presidency for himself, saw an opportunity. Ever since the Querétaro convention, relations between Carranza and Obregón had been cool.

General Venustiano Carranza at work at his desk in Durango, Mexico, on June 11, 1914. He became provisional president of Mexico following the overthrow of the dictatorial Huerta regime that summer. During his administration, the current constitution of Mexico was drafted.

At Querétaro, Obregón, eager to show the Mexican public that he could be an effective political as well as military leader, had spearheaded the drive to include progressive social reforms in the constitution, despite Carranza's objections. Yet, even though he had defied Carranza's wishes at the Constitutional Convention to enhance his own political reputation, Obregón had clung to the hope that the president, in gratitude for his critical role in Pancho Villa's defeat, would still back him in the 1920 elections.

Carranza, who would have run for reelection if the new constitution had not prohibited presidents from serving more than one term, wanted a successor he could readily manipulate from behind the scenes. Clearly, that man was not the ambitious and independent-minded Obregón. After Obregón announced his candidacy for president in June 1919, therefore, Carranza not only declined to endorse his former general, but he threw his support behind the candidacy of his loyal subordinate, the ambassador to the United States, Ignacio Bonillas.

By early 1920, to Carranza's dismay, there was little doubt that Obregón would prevail at the polls over the unpopular president's handpicked candidate, Bonillas. In April, with the elections just two months away, Carranza suddenly ordered Obregón to travel from his home state of Sonora to Mexico City to testify in the treason trial of an army colonel, a man whom Obregón had never even met. On April 23, suspecting that Carranza planned to have him imprisoned before the elections, Obregón—with the backing of two powerful fellow Sonorans, Governor Adolfo de la Huerta and General Plutarco Elías Calles—called on the Mexican people to rise up in arms against their president.

CARRANZA'S DOWNFALL

The slow pace of social reform under Carranza, his apparent complicity in the murder of Zapata, and his thinly veiled efforts to get Obregón out of the way before the national elections had caused the president to lose the respect of much of the Mexican populace. Obregón, in contrast, enjoyed broader popular support than ever before as well as the firm backing of the upper echelons of the Federal Army, who strongly preferred to have a former general in the National Palace as opposed to someone with no military background, like Bonillas. On May 7, realizing that his situation was hopeless yet still unwilling to resign, Carranza fled the capital for Veracruz, accompanied by a large entourage of supporters and family members. In Veracruz he planned to set up a government-in-exile, just as he had done in late 1914 when Villista and Zapatista troops were closing in on Mexico City.

As Carranza's train chugged toward the port city, it came under repeated attacks by insurgents. On May 14, the train trip came to an abrupt end at the Alijibes railway station in the state of Puebla because rebels had torn up the tracks beyond that point. Leaving most of his entourage behind in Alijibes, Carranza fled into Puebla's rugged hills on horseback, reaching the tiny hamlet of Tlaxcalantongo on May 20. At the invitation of a seemingly loyal local chieftain, General Rodolfo Herrero, Carranza decided to spend the night there in a peasant hut. At 4:00 A.M. the following morning, several armed men burst into the hut shouting, "¡*Viva Obregón!*" and "¡*Muerta Carranza!*" ("Death to Carranza!")[5] After shooting the president repeatedly at point-blank range, the gunmen escaped into the hills. No concrete evidence linking Obregón to the murder of his rival was ever uncovered. Nonetheless, Carranza's supporters could not help but note that General Herrero, who had clearly orchestrated the assassination, was never convicted of any crime.

Shortly after Carranza's funeral in Mexico City, Congress convened to choose an interim president to finish the slain leader's term. Obregón made no effort to secure the position for himself since even interim presidents were not allowed to succeed themselves, according to the strict provisions of the new constitution. Instead, Obregón backed his close Sonoran ally, Governor Adolfo de la Huerta, for the post. He also agreed to put off the presidential elections, originally scheduled for a few weeks after de la Huerta's appointment, until the end of the summer. To no one's surprise, Obregón won the election, held on September 5, by a landslide. Three months later, on December 1, 1920, he was inaugurated in a midnight ceremony at the Congressional Hall in Mexico City. Mexico had entered a new era. Because it finally brought to a close the widespread violence and deadly political rivalries that had rent the nation for nearly a decade, Obregón's inauguration has generally been viewed as the end of the Mexican Revolution.

8

The Mexican Revolution's Aftermath

The Mexican Revolution touched virtually every family in the republic at some point between its eruption in November 1910 and its traditional ending date on Álvaro Obregón's inauguration in December 1920. An estimated 1 million to 1.5 million Mexicans out of a total population of 15 million died as a consequence of the revolution, some 250,000 of them in battle and many thousands more through execution or massacre. Most of the remaining victims succumbed to typhus, smallpox, influenza, and other infectious diseases, which quickly spread through a population weakened by food shortages and nearly incessant violence. In light of the devastating toll a decade of war had exacted, President Obregón decided that protecting the country's still fragile peace and rebuilding its shattered economy, rather than enacting the revolutionary social reforms called for in the Constitution of 1917, must be his top priorities.

Obregón proceeded cautiously with the reforms set forth in the 1917 Constitution. He distributed just 3 million acres (1.2 million ha) of public and privately owned land among a total of 600 Indian villages, a figure that in no way reflected the far-reaching land redistribution program described in Article 27. Fearful of sparking an open conflict with Mexico's powerful Roman Catholic Church, Obregón largely ignored the constitution's controversial clauses regarding separation of church and state. He also made few meaningful concessions to Mexican workers during his administration, despite the constitution's strongly pro-labor provisions.

During Obregón's third year in office, Pancho Villa, the last of the great revolutionary leaders aside from the president himself, was assassinated. Whether Obregón had any part in his old enemy's demise remains unknown. Shortly after Carranza's murder in May 1920, Villa had accepted interim president Adolfo de la Huerta's generous offer of a large hacienda in Durango in exchange for laying down his arms. Villa kept his part of the bargain and lived quietly on his vast new estate. Even so, Villa, who had made many enemies—personal as well as political—over the years, was the target of several failed assassination attempts in the early 1920s. On the morning of July 23, 1923, while Villa was driving home from Chihuahua to his ranch, his luck finally ran out. As Villa's Dodge touring car slowed for a sharp turn, eight gunmen opened fire on the automobile from a nearby house, killing the 45-year-old former general and his five bodyguards almost instantly.

Jesús Salas Barrazas, a local Durango politician with a long-standing personal grudge against Villa, publicly claimed credit for arranging his assassination. Government officials, however, showed remarkably little interest in punishing Barrazas or any of his accomplices for the crime. After just three months in prison, Barrazas received an official pardon from Chihuahua's governor, and none of the eight triggermen was ever charged in connection with the shooting. The fact that Villa's killers man-

WOMEN IN THE MEXICAN REVOLUTION

Tens of thousands of Mexican women attached themselves to rebel armies as well as government forces during the Mexican Revolution. Dubbed *soldaderas*, they served as spies, scouts, and, on occasion, as armed combatants. The vast majority, however, followed husbands or boyfriends to war as companions and helpmates. Since none of the armies of the revolutionary era, not even the Federal Army, provided a quartermaster corps, the women acted as food gatherers, cooks, laundresses, and nurses for their significant others and sometimes for their menfolk's comrades-in-arms as well.

The life of the soldadera was not an easy one. "The soldaderas endured the hardships of the campaign without special consideration," note historians Michael Meyer, William Sherman, and Susan Deeds. "While the men were generally mounted, the women most often walked, carrying bedding, pots and pans, food, firearms, ammunition, and children. Often the men would gallop on ahead, engage the enemy in battle, and then rest. By the time the women caught up, they were ready to move again."* An especially large number of female camp followers accompanied Pancho Villa's División del Norte. Typically the women trudged along on foot behind the army's big cavalry force. When Villa used hijacked trains to transport his soldiers quickly from city to city, however, the soldaderas and their

aged to escape prosecution has led some historians to conclude that Obregón was the true mastermind behind his old foe's violent end. Among them is Frank McLynn, who contends in

children happily hitched rides on the trains' roofs or rode "under the railroad cars on planks tied with knots," according to one eyewitness account.**

Although Villa's own attitude toward women's proper role was "the traditional 'children, church and kitchen' of time-honored Mexican machismo," notes Frank McLynn, some soldaderas who accompanied the División del Norte took up arms and fought on the battlefield, usually disguised as males.*** The best known of these female warriors was Petra Herrera, who served as a line soldier for Villa under the male alias "Pedro Herrera" during the struggle to overthrow Victoriano Huerta. Once "Pedro" had established a reputation as a skilled and courageous fighter, Herrera decided to reveal the truth about her gender to Villa and ask him for a promotion. When Villa refused to even consider the idea of placing a woman in charge of male soldiers, she left the División del Norte and formed her own all-female rebel brigade. The brigade, which included 300 to 400 troops according to some contemporary accounts, carried out a number of successful guerrilla attacks on federal targets in northern Mexico.

* Michael C. Meyer, William L. Sherman, and Susan M. Deeds, *The Course of Mexican History*. New York: Oxford University Press, 1999, p. 535.

** Quoted in Elizabeth Salas, *Soldaderas in the Mexican Military: Myth and History*. Austin: University of Texas Press, 1990, p. 43.

*** Frank McLynn, *Villa and Zapata: A History of the Mexican Revolution*. New York: Carroll & Graf Publishers, 2000, p. 209.

Pancho Villa was assassinated in his car on July 23, 1923. While no one has ever proven who was responsible for the assassination, many historians believe his death was the result of a conspiracy between Plutarco Elías Calles and Joaquin Amaro, with the tacit approval of President Álvaro Obregón.

his biography of Villa that "a mountain of evidence, both documentary and memoir, implicates Obregón in the plot."[1]

A CATHOLIC REVOLT AND YET ANOTHER ASSASSINATION

Barred by the constitution from running for reelection in 1924, Obregón successfully backed Plutarco Elías Calles, a close ally in his revolt against Carranza, as his successor.

Like Obregón, Calles was more interested in preserving the peace and strengthening the national economy than in implementing the constitution's more radical provisions. The sole exception to this rule was in the area of religious reform. Determined to break the power of Mexico's wealthy and influential Catholic Church, Calles vigorously enforced the constitution's anticlerical clauses, including the bans on church involvement in primary education and voting by priests. In retaliation, church leaders suspended all public religious ceremonies, sparking a popular uprising known as the Cristero Rebellion in several strongly Catholic states in western Mexico. The bloody rebellion dragged on from 1927 until the summer of 1929, when U.S. Ambassador Dwight Morrow helped broker an agreement between church leaders and the Mexican government.

While the Cristero Rebellion was raging in western Mexico, Obregón decided that he wanted to be president again, even though the constitution restricted presidents to one term. At his urging, Obregón's supporters in Congress rammed through a constitutional amendment permitting nonconsecutive presidential terms in early 1928. On July 1 of that year, Obregón handily won the national elections. As it turned out, he would never see his second inauguration day. Like Madero, Carranza, Zapata, Villa, and virtually every other major figure of the Mexican Revolution, Álvaro Obregón was not destined to die peacefully in his bed of old age. On July 17, 1928, while the 48-year-old president-elect was celebrating his victory at a Mexico City restaurant, a young Catholic fanatic with ties to the Cristero rebels approached Obregón's table and shot him five times in the head at point-blank range.

LÁZARO CÁRDENAS'S REVOLUTIONARY REFORMS

At Calles's urging, Congress appointed his close associate, Emilio Portes Gil, as provisional president after Obregón's assassination. Although supposedly retired from politics, the

Plutarco Elías Calles *(with top hat in hand)* on the day he took the oath of office as president of Mexico in Mexico City in December 1924. Here, Calles is shown with ex-president Álvaro Obregón *(wearing glasses)*, who would be assassinated shortly after again winning the presidency in 1928.

following year Calles founded the powerful Partido Nacional Revolucionario (National Revolutionary Party) or PNR, which would rule Mexico for the next seven decades (from 1946 on, under the name, Partido Revolucionario Institucional). Working behind the scenes, he also continued to shape government policy during the brief interim presidencies of Portes Gil, Pascual Ortiz Rubio (1930–1932), and Abelardo L. Rodríguez (1932–1934). Under Calles's influence, the pace of social reform in Mexico remained slow through the early

1930s, while the central government focused on updating and expanding the country's infrastructure, particularly its roads and telephone network.

In 1934, Calles backed a relatively unknown politician and army officer named Lázaro Cárdenas in the first popular presidential elections to be held since Obregón's murder. Calles fully expected Mexico's new chief executive to do his bidding, just as Portes Gil, Rubio, and Rodríguez had done. But to Calles's consternation, it quickly became clear that Cárdenas was his own man. A firm believer in the principles of social justice and equality, Cárdenas was resolved to turn the revolutionary ideals of the 1917 Constitution into reality. When Calles publicly criticized his social and economic policies for veering too far to the left, Cárdenas shocked the former president by having him arrested and sent into exile.

As president, Cárdenas made agrarian reform his top priority. During his six-year term, he oversaw the redistribution of 45 million acres (18 million ha) of public and private land to Mexico's peasantry, most of it in the form of ejidos. This was more than five times as much land as Carranza, Obregón, and Calles together had dispersed during their administrations. As firm a supporter of organized labor as of the peasantry, Cárdenas also reorganized the PNR to give union leaders more say in Mexico's leading political party. In 1938, in the midst of a bitter wage dispute between striking oil workers and their American and British employers, he nationalized foreign-owned oil companies throughout Mexico, using Article 27 of the Constitution as the legal basis for his bold policy. A special government agency, Petróleos Mexicanos (Mexican Petroleum) or Pemex, was created to oversee the newly nationalized industry.

THE MEXICAN REVOLUTION'S LEGACY

After Cárdenas's presidential term ended in 1940, his more conservative successors gradually abandoned many of the revolutionary principles set forth in the 1917 Constitution.

The social reforms pushed by Cárdenas, including large-scale land redistribution and rural school construction, were expensive, and both agricultural and industrial production declined under his tenure. Hoping to reverse that trend and put Mexico back on a surer economic footing, a new generation of political leaders stressed industrialization and the development of commercial agriculture over the demands of the revolution's foot soldiers and staunchest supporters: poor farmers and workers. Even as Mexico's leaders paid lip service to the ideals of Zapata and other revered revolutionary heroes, they were backing away from the revolutionaries' core demands for social equality and a basic minimum standard of living for all Mexicans.

Although no Mexican president since Lázaro Cárdenas has ever shared his deep commitment to the revolutionaries' egalitarian vision, the Revolution of 1910–1920 nonetheless transformed Mexican society and culture in significant and lasting ways. Nowhere was the role of the revolution as an agent of social change more evident than in the area of land ownership. The Mexican masses, notes Michael Gonzales, had "rebelled, above all, to get land—in many cases, the same land that had been taken from them by hacendados during their lifetimes."[2] The comprehensive land redistribution program inspired by the revolution, which by the end of Cárdenas's term had dispersed tens of millions of acres to rural Indian communities, was the most far-reaching agrarian reform scheme to be instituted in the history of the Americas. Land ownership by foreigners and the Catholic Church plummeted and the nation's chief economic unit—the hacienda—vanished along with the aristocratic hacendado class that had long dominated the Mexican countryside.

Without question, rural society in Mexico was forever changed by the sweeping land reforms set down in the Constitution of 1917 and energetically carried out by the country's most genuinely revolutionary president, Lázaro Cárdenas, during the 1930s. Yet, even while the revolution was still being fought, it was helping to transform Mexican social and cultural life. The violence, famine, disease epidemics, and economic chaos of the war years, particularly in northern Mexico where most of the fighting occurred, spurred thousands of Mexicans to leave their ancestral villages in search of employment and a safer environment for themselves and their families. From 1910 to 1920, an estimated 250,000 war refugees fled across the border into the United States.

During the same period, hundreds of thousands of other Mexicans in war-torn regions moved from one part of their homeland to another. As a result of this mass internal migration, a new sense of national identity developed among Mexicans, and long-standing local cultural practices and attitudes regarding work, religion, and gender relations were transformed. The demographic upheavals of the revolutionary era meant that "northerners and southerners came into more frequent contact with one another, and distinct regional language patterns began to yield to a more homogeneous national tongue," write Meyer, Sherman, and Deeds. "Increased travel ... provided a broader conception and deeper appreciation of Mexico. Greater physical mobility brought about by war tended to increase miscegenation [intermarriage between races] and began to homogenize previously isolated zones."[3]

Another important cultural legacy of the Mexican Revolution lay in the realm of the arts. The revolution's emphasis on social and political equality for all Mexicans, including especially its overwhelmingly Indian peasantry, released a flood of creative energy among the country's artists and writers. The most famous and influential outlet for that energy came through the Mexican muralist movement that began in 1920 and peaked in the 1930s. As part of the movement, radical mural painters such as David Siqueiros, José Clemente Orozco, and, above all, Diego Rivera, brought Mexican art worldwide attention and acclaim through their vivid portrayals of Mexico's dramatic and sometimes painful history. Through their huge, colorful frescoes in Mexico City's National Palace and other public buildings, Rivera, Orozco, and Siqueiros sought to educate and uplift the masses by celebrating Mexico's pre-conquistador Indian past and populist revolutionary leaders and reformers such as Emiliano Zapata.

Although the Mexican Revolution fell far short of ending poverty and social inequality in Mexico, it did lay the groundwork for historic reforms that have had an enduring effect on the country's culture and society. Because of the revolution, dispossessed Indian communities received millions of acres of farmland, workers were legally guaranteed a minimum wage and the right to organize, foreign-owned oil companies were nationalized, and public education, particularly in rural areas, was greatly expanded. Although much of the revolutionaries' ambitious social agenda has yet to be fulfilled, the Mexico that emerged from the Revolution of 1910–1920 was very definitely not the Mexico of Porfirio Díaz.

CHRONOLOGY

1876	Porfirio Díaz becomes president of Mexico.
1884	After not running for reelection in 1880, Díaz is again elected president.
1890	Díaz pressures the legislature to pass a constitutional amendment allowing an individual to serve an unlimited number of successive presidential terms.
1908	In an interview, Díaz says he will not run in the 1910 election, but he has no intention of keeping that promise.
1910	**April** Francisco Madero enters the presidential race against Díaz. **July** After having Madero imprisoned, Díaz "wins" the presidential election. **November 20** The Mexican Revolution begins, pitting Madero's supporters against Díaz.
1911	**May** Madero's followers are victorious in the Battle of Ciudad Juárez. Díaz resigns the presidency and flees to Europe. **October** Madero is elected president. **November** Emiliano Zapata's Plan of Ayala, opposing Madero, is published.
1913	**February** Ten Tragic Days (Decena Trágica) standoff in Mexico City. General Victoriano Huerta seizes power and has Madero assassinated.

1913   March Venustiano Carranza forms Constitutionalist army to fight Huerta.

1914   April-November U.S. forces occupy the Mexican port city of Veracruz.

June Virtually all of Mexico has fallen under rebel control.

July Huerta resigns presidency and flees Mexico; Carranza names himself provisional president.

November Convention of Aguascalientes fails to unite revolutionaries.

1915   April-November Carranza's army defeats rebel Pancho Villa in a series of battles.

TIMELINE

1876
Porfirio Díaz becomes president of Mexico.

1911
Díaz resigns the presidency and flees to Europe.
October Madero is elected president.

1876

1913

1910
April Francisco Madero enters the presidential race against Díaz.
November 20 The Mexican Revolution begins, pitting Madero's supporters against Díaz.

1913
February Ten Tragic Days (Decena Trágica) standoff in Mexico City.
1913 General Victoriano Huerta seizes power and has Madero assassinated.
March
Venustiano Carranza forms Constitutionalist army to fight Huerta.

1916   **March** Villa's followers raid Columbus, New Mexico, after U.S. recognition of Carranza.

Unsuccessful U.S. Punitive Expedition to capture Villa begins.

By late 1916, much of Mexico is under Constitutionalist control.

1917   **February** Mexican Constitution of 1917 is approved.

May Carranza is officially sworn in as Mexico's first president under the new constitution.

1919   **April** Zapata is assassinated on Carranza's orders.

July 1914
Huerta resigns presidency and flees Mexico.

1917
February Mexican Constitution of 1917 is approved.
March Carranza is sworn in as Mexico's first president under the new constitution.

1914

1920

April–November 1915
Carranza's army defeats rebel Pancho Villa in a series of battles.

1920
April Obregón calls on Mexicans to take up arms against Carranza.
December Obregón is inaugurated as president: traditional ending date for the Mexican Revolution.

1919	**June** The Constitutionalist general Álvaro Obregón announces his presidential candidacy.
1920	**April** Obregón calls on Mexicans to take up arms against Carranza. **May** Carranza is assassinated after fleeing Mexico City. **December** Obregón is inaugurated as president: traditional ending date for the Mexican Revolution.
1923	**July** Villa is assassinated.
1928	Obregón wins a second term as president but is assassinated before he can take office.
1934-1940	The progressive reformer Lázaro Cárdenas serves as president, instituting many provisions contained in the Constitution of 1917.

NOTES

CHAPTER 1

1. Quoted in Eileen Welsome, *The General and the Jaguar: Pershing's Hunt for Pancho Villa.* New York: Little, Brown and Company, 2006, p. 19.

CHAPTER 2

1. Michael J. Gonzales, *The Mexican Revolution: 1910–1940.* Albuquerque: University of New Mexico Press, 2002, p. 11.
2. Quoted in Frank McLynn, *Villa and Zapata: A History of the Mexican Revolution.* New York: Carroll & Graf Publishers, 2000, p. 6.
3. Quoted in Paul Garner, *Porfirio Díaz.* London: Longman, 2001, p. 93.
4. Quoted in McLynn, *Villa and Zapata*, p. 6.
5. Gonzales, *The Mexican Revolution*, p. 13.
6. McLynn, *Villa and Zapata*, p. 6.
7. Quoted in Michael C. Meyer and William H. Beezley, *The Oxford History of Mexico.* New York: Oxford University Press, 2000, p. 404.
8. Quoted in Garner, *Porfirio Díaz*, p. 85.
9. Quoted in Meyer and Beezley, *The Oxford History of Mexico*, p. 403.
10. Gonzales, *The Mexican Revolution*, p. 15.

11. Adolfo Gilly, *The Mexican Revolution.* New York: The New Press, 2005, p. 21.
12. Gonzales, *The Mexican Revolution*, p. 29.
13. Thomas E. Skidmore and Peter H. Smith, *Modern Latin America.* New York: Oxford University Press, 2001, p. 226.

CHAPTER 3

1. McLynn, *Villa and Zapata*, p. 21.
2. Ibid., p. 24.
3. Quoted in Michael C. Meyer, William L. Sherman, and Susan M. Deeds, *The Course of Mexican History.* New York: Oxford University Press, 1999, p. 475.
4. Quoted in Garner, *Porfirio Díaz*, p. 194.
5. Gonzales, *The Mexican Revolution*, p. 71.
6. McLynn, *Villa and Zapata*, pp. 22–23.
7. Ibid., p. 25.
8. Welsome, *The General and the Jaguar*, p. 18.
9. Quoted in Gonzales, *The Mexican Revolution*, p. 73.
10. Quoted in Meyer, Sherman, and Deeds, *The Course of Mexican History*, p. 482.
11. Ibid., p. 482.
12. Meyer and Beezley, *The Oxford History of Mexico*, p. 411.

13. Quoted in Meyer, Sherman, and Deeds, *The Course of Mexican History*, p. 487.

CHAPTER 4

1. Quoted in Gonzales, *The Mexican Revolution*, p. 82.
2. Ibid., p. 87.
3. Meyer, Sherman, and Deeds, *The Course of Mexican History*, pp. 494–495.
4. Quoted in John Womack Jr., *Zapata and the Mexican Revolution.* New York: Vintage Books, 1968, p. 96.
5. McLynn, *Villa and Zapata*, p. 131.
6. Ibid., p. 131.
7. Welsome, *The General and the Jaguar*, p. 26.
8. Gonzales, *The Mexican Revolution*, p. 94.
9. Meyer and Beezley, *The Oxford History of Mexico*, p. 444.
10. Quoted in Welsome, *The General and the Jaguar*, p. 30.

CHAPTER 5

1. Quoted in Welsome, *The General and the Jaguar*, p. 33.
2. John S.D. Eisenhower, *Intervention! The United States and the Mexican Revolution, 1913–1917.* New York: W.W. Norton, 1993, p. 52.
3. Quoted in Friedrich Katz, *The Life and Times of Pancho Villa.* Palo Alto, Calif.: Stanford University Press, 1998, p. 205.
4. Eisenhower, *Intervention!*, p. 50.

5. Quoted in Womack, *Zapata*, p. 221.
6. Quoted in Eisenhower, *Intervention!*, p. 51.
7. Quoted in Welsome, *The General and the Jaguar*, p. 33.
8. Quoted in Womack, *Zapata*, pp. 168–169.
9. Quoted in Meyer, Sherman, and Deeds, *The Course of Mexican History*, p. 508.
10. Quoted in Katz, *The Life and Times of Pancho Villa*, p. 310.
11. Quoted in Welsome, *The General and the Jaguar*, p. 32.
12. Ibid., p. 43.

CHAPTER 6

1. Quoted in Eisenhower, *Intervention!*, p. 159.
2. Quoted in Meyer, Sherman, and Deeds, *The Course of Mexican History*, p. 518.
3. Quoted in Womack, *Zapata*, p. 222.
4. Gonzales, *The Mexican Revolution*, p. 136.
5. Welsome, *The General and the Jaguar*, p. 56.
6. Gonzales, *The Mexican Revolution*, p. 152.
7. Quoted in Meyer, Sherman, and Deeds, *The Course of Mexican History*, p. 520.
8. McLynn, *Villa and Zapata*, p. 324.
9. Gonzales, *The Mexican Revolution*, p. 156.
10. Quoted in Meyer and Beezley, *The Oxford History of Mexico*, p. 460.

CHAPTER 7

1. All quotations from the Mexican Constitution are from the "1917 Constitution of Mexico," http://www.ilstu.edu/class/hist263/docs/1917const.html#TitleI.

2. Meyer, Sherman, and Deeds, *The Course of Mexican History*, p. 526.

3. Ibid., p. 528.

4. Meyer and Beezley, *The Oxford History of Mexico*, p. 463.

5. Quoted in Eisenhower, *Intervention!*, p. 319.

CHAPTER 8

1. McLynn, *Villa and Zapata*, p. 395.

2. Gonzales, *The Mexican Revolution*, p. 262.

3. Meyer, Sherman, and Deeds, *The Course of Mexican History*, p. 544.

BIBLIOGRAPHY

Eisenhower, John S.D. *Intervention! The United States and the Mexican Revolution, 1913–1917*. New York: W.W. Norton, 1993.

Garner, Paul. *Porfirio Díaz*. London: Longman, 2001.

Gilly, Adolfo. *The Mexican Revolution*. New York: The New Press, 2005.

Gonzales, Michael J. *The Mexican Revolution, 1910–1940*. Albuquerque: University of New Mexico Press, 2002.

Katz, Friedrich. *The Life and Times of Pancho Villa*. Palo Alto, Calif.: Stanford University Press, 1998.

Knight, Alan. *The Mexican Revolution, 1910–1920*, 2 vols. Cambridge: Cambridge University Press, 1986.

McLynn, Frank. *Villa and Zapata: A History of the Mexican Revolution*. New York: Carroll & Graf Publishers, 2000.

Meyer, Michael C., and William H. Beezley. *The Oxford History of Mexico*. New York: Oxford University Press, 2000.

Meyer, Michael C., William L. Sherman, and Susan M. Deeds. *The Course of Mexican History*. New York: Oxford University Press, 1999.

Salas, Elizabeth. *Soldaderas in the Mexican Military: Myth and History*. Austin: University of Texas Press, 1990.

Skidmore, Thomas E., and Peter H. Smith. *Modern Latin America*. New York: Oxford University Press, 2001.

Welsome, Eileen. *The General and the Jaguar: Pershing's Hunt for Pancho Villa*. New York: Little, Brown and Company, 2006.

Womack, John, Jr. *Zapata and the Mexican Revolution*. New York: Vintage Books, 1968.

FURTHER RESOURCES

BOOKS

Carroll, Bob. *Pancho Villa*. San Diego: Lucent Books, 1996.

Foster, Lynn V. *A Brief History of Mexico*. New York: Facts on File, 2004.

Frost, Mary Pierce, and Susan Keegan. *The Mexican Revolution*. San Diego: Lucent Books, 1997.

Jowett, Philip, and Alejandro de Quesada. *The Mexican Revolution, 1910–20*. Oxford, U.K.: Osprey, 2006.

Stein, R. Conrad. *The Mexican Revolution, 1910–1920*. New York: New Discovery, 1994.

WEB SITES

1917 Constitution of Mexico
http://www.ilstu.edu/class/hist263/docs/1917const.html

Emiliano Zapata: EmersonKent.com
http://www.emersonkent.com/history_notes/emiliano_zapata.htm

In Pursuit of Pancho Villa: 1916–1917
http://www.hsgng.org/pages/pancho.htm

Mexconnect: The Mexican Revolution of 1910
http://www.mexconnect.com/articles/2824-the-mexican-revolution-1910

The Mexican Revolution
http://www.fsmitha.com/h2/ch03mex.htm

The Mexican Revolution
http://www.latinamericanstudies.org/mex-revolution.htm

PICTURE CREDITS

INDEX

ABOUT THE AUTHOR

LOUISE CHIPLEY SLAVICEK received her master's degree in history from the University of Connecticut. She is the author of numerous articles on American and world history for scholarly journals and young people's magazines, including *Cobblestone* and *Calliope*. Her more than two-dozen books for young people include *Women of the American Revolution*, *Israel*, *Carlos Santana*, and *The Chinese Cultural Revolution*. She lives in Ohio with her husband, Jim, a research biologist, and their two children, Krista and Nathan.